PUFFIN BOOKS

DAKOTA of the WHITE FLATS

Philip Ridley was born in the East End of London, where he still lives and works. He studied painting at St Martin's School of Art and has exhibited widely throughout Europe. He has written three books for adults, *Crocodilia*, *In the Eyes of Mr Fury* and *Flamingoes in Orbit*, as well as the highly acclaimed screenplay for *The Krays* feature film. He also wrote and directed his own film, *The Reflecting Skin*, which has won eleven international awards. As well as radio plays for the BBC, he has written three successful stage plays, *The Pitchfork Disney*, *The Fastest Clock in the Universe* and *Ghost from a Perfect Place*. He has written four other novels for children, *Mercedes Ice*, *Krindlekrax* (for which he won the Smarties Prize for Children's Fiction and the W. H. Smith Mind-Boggling Books Award), *Meteorite Spoon* and *Kasper in the Glitter*.

Other books by Philip Ridley in Puffin

KASPER IN THE GLITTER
KRINDLEKRAX
MERCEDES ICE
METEORITE SPOON
SCRIBBLEBOY
ZINDERZUNDER

for younger readers

DREAMBOAT ZING

Philip Ridley

DAKOTA of the WHITE FLATS

Illustrated by Chris Riddell

PUFFIN BOOKS

PUFFIN BOOKS

Published by the Penguin Group
Penguin Books Ltd, 27 Wrights Lane, London W8 5TZ, England
Penguin Books USA Inc., 375 Hudson Street, New York, New York 10014, USA
Penguin Books Australia Ltd, Ringwood, Victoria, Australia
Penguin Books Canada Ltd, 10 Alcorn Avenue, Toronto, Ontario, Canada M4V 3B2
Penguin Books (NZ) Ltd, 182–190 Wairau Road, Auckland 10, New Zealand

Penguin Books Ltd, Registered Offices: Harmondsworth, Middlesex, England

First published by Wiliam Collins Sons & Co. Ltd 1989
This edition published by Viking 1995
Published in Puffin Books 1996

7

Text copyright © Philip Ridley, 1989
Illustrations copyright © Chris Riddell, 1995
All rights reserved

Filmset in Palatino

Made and printed in England by Clays Ltd, St Ives plc

For Helge –
our friendship is a constant adventure

— 1 —

Dakota Pink was woken by screaming.

The screams came from the bathroom as Henry saw the silverfish. Silverfish are the tiny caterpillar-like creatures that live behind the sink. During the night they come out and in the morning they scarper over the tiles.

Henry Twig lodged with Dakota and her mother. He was tall, thin, twenty-eight years old and . . . very afraid of silverfish.

Usually Dakota, who was ten years old and very afraid of nothing, would get up and clear away the silverfish. But today, Sunday, she was determined to stay in bed. She had been working hard on the market stall the day before. Henry didn't have a job. The most strenuous thing he did was pick his teeth with a golden toothpick.

I'm not getting up, Dakota thought. Henry can scream all he likes, but I'm staying in bed.

Henry rushed into Dakota's room trembling with fear.

Henry's hair was thick, black and slicked smooth with handfuls of grease. If he wasn't greasing his hair, then he was brushing his black suit or starching his white shirt or polishing his shoes. Henry was the vainest person in the White Flats.

The White Flats were four buildings that faced each other across a concrete square. Although they were called the White Flats they weren't white at all. They were a dirty yellow colour, covered with gigantic cracks like veins. Dakota, her mother and Henry Twig lived in a ground-floor flat.

Dakota sat up in bed and looked at Henry, who was wearing silk pyjamas and a hairnet.

'There's an army of silverfish in the bathroom,' Henry cried.

'Don't be a baby,' Dakota told him.

'Please get rid of them for me,' Henry pleaded.

'No,' said Dakota. 'I'm tired.'

'But you always do it,' Henry said.

'Then it's about time I stopped.'

Henry didn't know what to do. He desperately wanted to go to the bathroom. For a few minutes he shuffled uncomfortably. Then . . .

'If you get rid of them,' Henry said, 'I'll give you something.'

'Give me what?' Dakota asked.

'Anything,' Henry said.

'Something from your room?' Dakota said.

In all the years Henry had been lodging with Dakota and her mother he had never let anyone into his room.

'All right,' Henry said, 'I agree. You can have something from my room. Just clear away the silverfish. Please, Dakota! Please!'

Dakota got out of bed, put on her dressing-gown, then

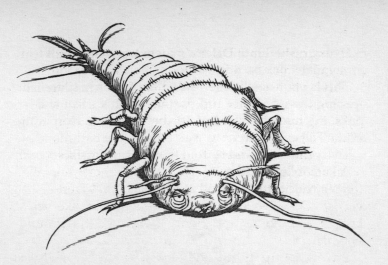

strolled down the hall to the bathroom.

There, on the floor, she saw twelve silverfish. All of them were large, but one of them, the one by the spider plant, was the biggest, fattest silverfish Dakota had ever seen.

Dakota swiftly caught all the other silverfish and flushed them down the toilet, but the one by the spider plant, so fat it could barely move, she put in her dressing-gown pocket.

'It's safe now,' she said to Henry, who was waiting outside. 'They're all gone.'

Henry rushed inside and slammed the door.

Dakota peeped in her pocket. The larger silverfish crawled over bits of fluff and tissue-paper. Dakota studied it carefully and gazed at its hairy legs, its gleaming, scaled back and fish-like face.

'I'm going to keep you,' said Dakota. 'You're going to be my pet.'

Dakota ran downstairs to the living-room, where her mother, Lucy, was asleep in the armchair, her Cocoon on Castors as she called it. Carefully, Dakota rummaged through her sleeping mother's pockets until she found a matchbox. She emptied the matches out and took the empty matchbox back to her room.

'This is your new home,' said Dakota to her silverfish, opening the matchbox and putting the silverfish inside.

For a while she listened to the silverfish scarpering around. Then she went to wait outside the bathroom.

Henry came out and started to walk towards his room.

Dakota followed him.

Henry turned and glared at Dakota.

'And where do you think you're going, young lady?' he asked.

'With you,' Dakota replied.

'And why's that, may I ask?'

'You said I could choose something from your room.'

'And why would I say something like that?' Henry sneered.

'Because I got rid of the silverfish for you,' Dakota said.

'Is that so?' said Henry. 'Well, let me tell you something, young lady. No one ever enters the room of Henry Twig.'

And with that he went into his room and slammed the door.

Dakota was furious. She should have been used to Henry by now – there was nothing he enjoyed more than tormenting her – but, somehow, his behaviour surprised her every time.

'If you don't give me something I'll spit on your shoes,' Dakota cried through the keyhole. 'Your uncomfortable, pointed black shoes. The ones that go clickitty-clackitty-click-clock when you walk. I'll spit on them, Henry. I'll spit on them –'

The door opened a little.

'All right, all right,' Henry said, because he knew Dakota spat a lot when she got angry. 'I'll give you something. But you can't come in. No one ever comes in. Now then, what do you want?'

Dakota thought for a while and said, 'Earrings!'

Henry's door closed. Then it opened again and he gave Dakota a pair of sparkling diamond earrings.

'Now take them and go away!' said Henry sharply.

Dakota tried to peer behind Henry's shoulder into his room. She saw things glistening and glimmering inside as if his room were full of treasure.

Then the door slammed shut.

2

Later that morning, at breakfast, Dakota showed the earrings to her mum.

'The trouble is,' said Dakota, 'I don't see how you put them on.'

'They're for pierced ears,' said her mum, 'and your ears haven't been pierced.'

'You mean pierced like Treacle's ears?' asked Dakota.

'That's right,' replied her mum. 'Just like little Treacle's ears.'

Treacle was Dakota's best friend. They both went to the same school and were interested in all the same things: insects, chocolate biscuits and the strange rumbling sounds bellies make when people get hungry.

Treacle's real name was Penelope Duck. Once, when she was only three years old, she had found a tin of treacle in the kitchen and eaten the whole lot. She was sick for days afterwards and had to go to hospital. From that moment on everyone called her Treacle and her real name was forgotten.

'Where can I get my ears pierced?' Dakota asked her mum.

'Oh, lots of places,' she replied. 'Why don't you try the jewellers on the corner? The jewellers where I bought the diamond as big as a pea.'

'That jewellers was knocked down ages ago, Mum,' Dakota said. 'And all the shops next to it. There's a supermarket there now.'

Lucy's eyes filled with tears. She rummaged in her dressing-gown pocket and pulled out a crumpled tissue to blow her nose.

'It's been so long,' wept Lucy, 'so very long.'

When Lucy said this she meant it had been so long since she last left the flat. Lucy had not left the flat since Dakota was one year old, and the reason for this is a man named Caleb Pink.

When Lucy had been eighteen years old she had met and fallen in love with Caleb Pink, the local roadsweeper. He was planning to be a famous writer one day. Or so he said.

'I'm working on my novel,' he would say, 'and when it's published it will sell a million copies. Perhaps even two million if they turn it into a film.'

Most people thought that Caleb was an idiot. But not Lucy. She thought he was a genius. She would watch him sweep the roads for hours and hours. No one held a broom like Caleb Pink.

Once or twice Lucy plucked up enough courage to talk to him. But Caleb would merely nod or grunt or, even worse, look straight through Lucy as though she wasn't there at all.

One day, while Lucy was watching Caleb sweep up some broken beer bottles, she noticed a sheet of paper fall out of his pocket. She rushed over to pick it up. The sheet of paper was covered in writing and on the top of the page it said:

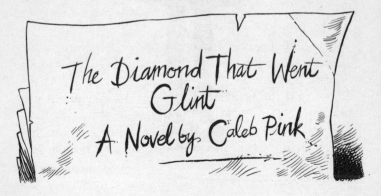

Lucy tapped Caleb on the shoulder and gave him the sheet of paper. He thanked her and explained it was the first page of his novel.

'Do you like diamonds?' Lucy asked.

'Yes,' Caleb replied curtly. 'I like diamonds a lot.'

'Big diamonds?' asked Lucy.

'Yes,' said Caleb. 'Big diamonds. They've got to be at least the size of a pea, otherwise I'm just not interested.'

Lucy went home and collected all the jewellery she had. It wasn't much: a pair of pearl earrings, a gold ring, a sovereign necklace and a bracelet with magic charms. She took all her jewellery to the pawn shop and got money for them. She put it in a shoebox under her bed and went out to look for a job.

Two days later she started work in the local launderette. She worked there all through the day and at night she swept the place clean. All the money she earned she put in the shoebox.

For two years Lucy worked and worked. She didn't go out, she hardly ate a thing, she didn't buy herself clothes or sweets. When the shoebox was full she took it to the jewellers and asked the jeweller which was the biggest diamond ring she could get for her money.

The jeweller counted the money, then went to the window display. When he returned he held a ring. He gave it to Lucy.

'Is this diamond big enough for you?' he asked.

'I think so,' replied Lucy. 'It is about the size of a pea, wouldn't you say?'

'Yes,' said the jeweller, nodding, 'it looks about pea-size to me.'

Lucy searched the streets for Caleb Pink. She found him outside the local pub, sweeping up some broken beer bottles.

'What do you want?' asked Caleb, glancing at Lucy. 'I'm

trying to do my work. Sweeping's a difficult job.'

Lucy held the diamond ring in front of Caleb's eyes.

Caleb stared at the ring. His mouth dropped open and his eyes grew wide.

'You can have it,' Lucy said softly.

Caleb dropped his broom.

'Do you like it?' Lucy asked.

Caleb tried to speak, but the sight of the diamond had taken his voice away.

'I said, do you like it?' asked Lucy again.

Caleb nodded.

'If you marry me,' said Lucy, 'I'll give it to you.'

Caleb reached out and took the ring. He gazed at it for a while, then put it on his finger and giggled with delight.

Lucy and Caleb were married the following day.

One year later Lucy gave birth to a baby girl. While the baby was being born, Caleb sat in the hospital waiting-room flicking through magazines. When the nurse came to tell him that he was now a father he looked down at a photograph in a magazine of golden fields, blue sky and distant mountains. It looked like paradise to Caleb. Beneath the photograph
were the words
NORTH DAKOTA.

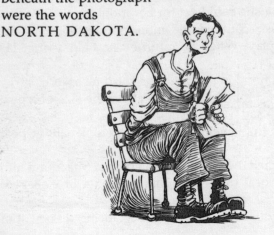

'That's what I'll call my child!' Caleb exclaimed. 'When my novel is published I'll earn lots of money. We'll all live in North Dakota and get away from these grotty White Flats once and for all.'

So Lucy and Caleb's baby girl was named Dakota.

Lucy bought Dakota a big, black pram with gleaming silver bits. The baby was put in the pram, but she cried non-stop.

The baby's crying annoyed Caleb.

'How can I be expected to write a novel with all that noise!' Caleb cried.

But write a novel he did.

Caleb sent it to a publisher.

The next day the novel was returned with a note.

The note said:

Dear Mr Pink

Thank you for letting us see your novel, but, quite frankly, we think it's the worst load of tripe we've ever had the misfortune of reading in all our years of publishing. You are obviously not a writer. To publish this would be a waste of a tree.

Don't bother us again.

The Publisher

Caleb read the letter
over and over again.
At first he was upset.
Then he was angry.
He decided to blame
baby Dakota.

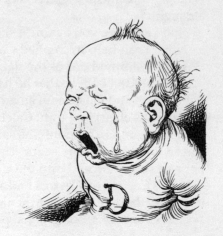

'It's that baby's fault!' he said to Lucy. 'How can I be expected to write a masterpiece with that thing crying. She makes me sick. Children make me feel sick!'

The next day, while he was walking down the street, Caleb saw two children skipping and, right then and there, he vomited. After that, Caleb felt sick if he saw anything to do with children: dolls, prams, jigsaw puzzles, nappies. And, in particular, cute children. Cute children made him feel sick for hours and hours and hours.

One day Caleb packed his suitcase.

'Where are you off to?' called Lucy.

'I'm leaving,' cried Caleb. 'Everything about this place makes me feel sick. It's exhausting me! I'm leaving you and the baby and the White Flats.'

'But you can't leave me!' cried Lucy.

'Why can't I?' asked Caleb.

'Because I gave you a diamond as big as a pea.'

'I don't care,' said Caleb. 'I'm leaving and that's that.'

'Give me back my diamond then!' demanded Lucy.

'No,' said Caleb. 'I'll take it with me and find my Dakota. And I mean the *place*, not that crying pipsqueak of a daughter.'

'Will I ever see you again?' asked Lucy.

'Not if I can help it,' replied Caleb.

And he stormed out of the flat.

Lucy couldn't believe that he had gone. She went to the living-room and fell back in an armchair. 'I'm never going to leave this chair! Not until Caleb comes back to me! This chair is as safe as a cocoon!' she said. And that's where she stayed for the next nine years. The armchair grew around her and slowly turned into the Cocoon on Castors.

Lucy's Cocoon on Castors had an upright lamp nailed to its back so that she could read at night. Down one side were two racks of books, some pens, pencils, a deck of cards, a

radio, a portable television, bottles of lemonade, balls of
wool and knitting-needles, magazines, a bowl of peanuts,
a kettle, a teapot and a packet of digestive biscuits.

Down the other side were three hot-water bottles, a clock, a torch, a potted plant, another television set, a few spare blankets, a telephone, a pair of binoculars, a gold-fish bowl without a goldfish, a small record-player and a large bag of salt-and-vinegar crisps.

Moving the armchair was made easier a couple of years ago when Henry attached electric motors to the castors and fixed a steering-wheel between Lucy's legs.

So now, whenever Dakota talks about buildings that have been knocked down, or things that have been changed, Lucy can't help but cry and feel sad.

'All those old places that I used to know being knocked down to make way for a supermarket. It's terrible.' The tears trickled down Lucy's cheeks. 'Oh, Dakota,' she wept, 'I need a dumpling. Make me a dumpling.'

Dakota kissed her mother and went into the kitchen. She put some flour and water into a bowl and started to make her mother's morning dumpling.

Dumplings were the only things that Lucy ate. In the morning she had a dumpling smothered with jam and whipped cream, in the afternoon she had a dumpling soaked in tomato sauce and pickle, and every evening she had three toasted dumplings with cheese and rashers of bacon.

When Dakota had finished making the dumpling she took it to her mother, then went back to her room. She noticed that some of the flour and water had got on to her nightdress and made it go stiff. It always amazed Dakota how flour and water could make things go hard as stone.

While she dressed she spoke to her silverfish.

'You're my own special pet,' said Dakota, 'and I love you.'

She opened the matchbox a fraction and looked inside. The silverfish looked up at her.

'Come on,' said Dakota, 'let's go and see Treacle.'

3

Treacle lived on the other side of the White Flats. To get there Dakota had to walk across a concrete square.

In the middle of the square was a broken water fountain. Once it had been beautiful, full of water-lilies and goldfish, but now it was piled high with rubbish and supermarket trolleys.

Supermarket trolleys were the main feature of the White Flats. They were scattered everywhere, like the skeletons of long-forgotten animals.

As Dakota walked across the square she caught sight of Medusa.

Medusa was a tall, thin woman with long green hair who sometimes stood in the middle of the square and called, 'Oscar! Oscar! I can't find it, Oscar!' What it was she couldn't find and who Oscar was, no one knew.

Medusa also took a great interest in everyone's jewellery. If someone was getting engaged or married, then Medusa had to look at the ring. No one knew why this happened. It was just a tradition of the White Flats.

Medusa's favourite colour was green. Apart from her green hair, she wore a green dress, green stockings, green shoes, green gloves and a green silk scarf. Although her clothes were old and torn and either bought in junk-shops or found in dustbins, Medusa acted as if she were a Hollywood movie star. She smoked her cigarettes in a long green cigarette holder, wore lots of make-up, and called all her neighbours 'darling'.

Wherever Medusa went she pushed a rusty supermarket trolley in front of her. The trolley was piled high with blankets and cabbage leaves. In the trolley, or so it was said, was Medusa's baby monster.

Dakota ran through the square to the opposite block of flats and knocked on Treacle's door.

Treacle opened it.

Treacle had short spiky blonde hair and a face full of freckles, quite different from Dakota, with her spiky black hair and a face so pale it seemed to glow in the dark.

Dakota showed Treacle her pet silverfish.

'Oh, it's marvellous,' said Treacle. 'It's about the size of . . . of . . . a quarter of a cherry.'

It was a habit of Treacle's to measure everything in terms of either fruit or vegetables. Here are some size evaluations according to Treacle, or measurements in 'Treacleze', as Dakota called them:

An ant is half a grape pip.

A dog is twelve cauliflowers.

A car is one thousand one hundred and ninety-seven melons.

A flat is three billion potatoes.

The White Flats are a zillion aubergines.

And now, to add to that, Dakota's pet silverfish was a quarter of a cherry.

Dakota was pleased to get its size in Treacleze.

'That's a good size,' said Dakota.

'A very good size,' agreed Treacle. 'Now, what are you going to call it?'

'I haven't thought of a name yet,' said Dakota. 'But I'm sure I'll think of one soon.'

'What does it eat?' asked Treacle.

'I'm not sure,' replied Dakota. 'It lives in the bathroom, so perhaps it lives on toothpaste.'

'Let's find out!' exclaimed Treacle.

She ran to the bathroom, found the toothpaste and gave it to Dakota.

Dakota squeezed a blob of paste into the matchbox. Immediately the silverfish crawled up and started to eat.

'I told you,' said Dakota triumphantly.

'It smells of toothpaste now,' said Treacle. 'All minty.'

Dakota looked at Treacle and smiled. 'That's what I'll call it,' she said.

'What?' asked Treacle.

'Minty!' said Dakota.

Treacle's mother came into the room.

'What are you two up to? More trouble?' she asked.

Dakota and Treacle hid the matchbox.

'Nothing,' Treacle said. 'Just talking.'

'Are you having dinner with us, Dakota?' asked Treacle's mum.

'Yes please,' said Dakota.

'Well, don't go far away,' said Treacle's mum, and went out of the room.

Because Dakota's mum was in the Cocoon on Castors, Dakota spent most of her time at Treacle's. And Treacle's mum, whose name was Pat, cooked nearly all of Dakota's meals and did her laundry as well.

It was on Pat's fruit and vegetable stall that both Dakota and Treacle worked every Saturday to get pocket money.

While Pat was preparing dinner Dakota said, 'I want to find out something.'

Every time Dakota said this, Treacle knew that it was going to be the start of an adventure.

'What do you want to find out?' asked Treacle.

'I want to find out what Medusa keeps in her supermarket trolley,' said Dakota. 'If it really is her baby monster, then I want to know.'

'But how are you going to find out?' asked Treacle.

'I have a plan,' said Dakota.

Treacle tingled all over.

'Oh, what?' she asked eagerly. 'What?'

'Look at these,' Dakota said, and took the earrings that Henry had given her from her pocket.

'Where did you get those?' asked Treacle.

'Henry gave them to me,' replied Dakota.

'Henry!' exclaimed Treacle, who knew how Henry tormented Dakota. 'Why?'

'Because I threatened not to clear away the silverfish this morning.'

'Is he still afraid of them?'

'Petrified.'

'He's such a big baby. I remember when he –'

'Oh, quiet, Treacle,' said Dakota. 'Now, do you want to hear my plan or not, you stupid toeflake?'

'Of course I do.'

'Then just park your lips for a while and listen,' said

Dakota. 'Now, during the week I'll get my ears pierced and start wearing these earrings. You mention this fact to Medusa.'

'*Talk* to her!' exclaimed Treacle, who was secretly afraid of the tall, thin woman with long green hair.

'Do you want to find out what's in her supermarket trolley or not?' asked Dakota impatiently.

'Of course I do,' said Treacle softly.

'Then shut up and do as you're told! Honestly, Treacle. Sometimes I wonder why I'm friends with you at all.'

'Oh, don't talk like that,' said Treacle, upset. 'I'll do whatever you say, you know that.'

'I should think so too,' said Dakota. 'Now listen. You tell old Medusa about my new earrings.'

'Then she'll want to have a look at them,' said Treacle.

'Exactly! But you'll have to make sure we time it right. I'll have my ears pierced on Thursday after I've made Mum her evening dumpling, then you'll have to tell Medusa on Friday, so she'll look at my earrings on Saturday.'

'Why Saturday?' asked Treacle.

'So she'll come up to me when I'm working on the stall with you,' explained Dakota.

'How does that help us?' asked Treacle.

'Oh, Treacle, really, I wish you had a brain. It's as obvious as the freckles on your face. While I show Medusa my earrings, you go to her supermarket trolley and rummage around in the cabbage leaves until you discover what's in there.'

Treacle took a deep breath and swallowed. She didn't like the sound of this plan at all. It seemed to her that she had to do all the work while Dakota did nothing. But she didn't say anything. Dakota would be annoyed if Treacle complained, and an angry Dakota was a terrible sight.

Instead, Treacle said, 'Anything you say, Dakota.'

'That's what I like to hear,' Dakota said. And then her voice turned to a whisper. 'You know something, Treacle, old fruit?'

'What?' asked Treacle.

'I hope it is a monster,' said Dakota softly. 'Really I do.'

4

The next Saturday morning Dakota made an extra large dumpling for her mum. She covered it with jam and whipped cream and then, as a special treat, stuck a bar of chocolate in the middle.

'You're spoiling me,' said Lucy. 'Is it my birthday or something?'

'No,' said Dakota. 'It's just that I'm in a good mood.'

'Oh dear,' said Lucy. 'I know what that means.'

'What?'

'It means you're going to start another adventure.'

'That's right,' said Dakota, smiling.

'But the last time you had an adventure you were gone for three days and three nights,' sighed Lucy. 'And all I could do was sit here in my Cocoon on Castors and get more and more worried.'

'Well, that was different,' explained Dakota. 'That was because I had to go in search of the loudest tummy rumble in the White Flats, and that took some finding. But this adventure won't take any time at all.'

'And why's that?' asked Lucy.

'Because this adventure is different. All I want to do is find out what Medusa has in her supermarket trolley.'

'Oh, Dakota,' sighed Lucy, holding her daughter's hand. 'Why don't you leave that poor old woman alone? She's suffered enough in her life.'

'I'm just curious,' said Dakota.

Dakota kissed her mum goodbye and rushed out of the house.

She ran down the street to the market and found Treacle on the fruit and veg stall.

Treacle was just putting out the apples. She was dressed in a blue overall, and woollen mittens to keep out the cold. Although it was May, the nights and mornings were still freezing. Treacle's lips and nose were blue and she was shivering so much her teeth rattled.

'Morning, Treacle,' said Dakota, putting on her overall and helping with the apples.

'I still think you're brave,' said Treacle.

'Brave about what?' asked Dakota.

'Getting your ears pierced.'

'Oh yes,' Dakota said, touching the diamond earrings in her ears, 'I was very brave. The pain was unbearable, but I didn't cry or complain. Not once.' Then she stared at Treacle. 'Did you tell Medusa about the earrings yesterday?' she asked.

'Yes,' Treacle replied. 'I told her just as I was throwing some rubbish into the broken water fountain.'

'And what did she say?'

'Nothing. She just smiled and nodded. But she knows you work with me on the stall today. You can be sure she'll come.'

Treacle's mother, Pat, came up. She was carrying a box of cabbages.

'Help me spread these cabbages out, Dakota,' said Pat.

Dakota took a couple of cabbages and started to put them on the vegetable section of the stall.

Pat bent down to pick up a handful of cabbages as well. As she did so a book fell out of her overall pocket.

It was the latest Lassitter Peach novel.

'Oh dear,' said Pat, brushing the book clean. 'Mustn't get it dirty. This is one of his best. Has your mum read this one, Dakota?'

Dakota stared at the novel. It was a typical Lassitter Peach cover: a woman dressed in flowing pink silk stood alone on a green hillside. In the distance were thatched cottages and sheep. There were tears in the woman's eyes and she was holding a letter. This novel was called *Love on a Day That Ended with Sunshine*.

'No,' said Dakota. 'I don't think she's read that one. She's got all the others though.'

There were over a hundred Lassitter Peach romances. Nearly everyone in the White Flats read them. People read them at bus-stops, in the launderette, while playing bingo, shopping, watching television. The novels were all about lonely women falling in love with charming men, and all the stories had happy endings.

'This one is so sad,' said Pat, putting the novel back into her pocket. 'But I'm sure it'll end happily. I'll have to lend it to your mum.'

For the rest of the morning Dakota thought about Lassitter Peach and his endless succession of romantic novels. Although he lived very close to the White Flats no one ever saw him because he was a recluse and afraid of germs. All the money he earned from his writing (which must be quite a lot as several of his books had been made into films) had been spent on buying himself an island. The island was called Dog Island and was in the middle of the river that ran behind the supermarket.

Lassitter Peach had built a house on Dog Island. Although hardly anyone had seen it close up (because of Lassitter Peach's fear of germs), it was reported to be like a fortress. One or two people had tried to break in because Lassitter was one of the richest men (if not *the* richest) in the world, but no one had succeeded.

Dakota was shaken out of her thoughts by Treacle tugging at her sleeve.

'What is it?' said Dakota angrily.

'It's her!' cried Treacle. 'Her!'

'What do you mean?' asked Dakota.

'It's her!' Treacle cried again. 'Medusa! Look!'

Dakota peered over Treacle's shoulder and saw Medusa approaching the stall.

'Right!' said Dakota. 'You know what to do!'

'Yes,' said Treacle nervously.

'Don't let me down,' warned Dakota.

'I won't,' said Treacle.

Dakota started to rearrange some cauliflowers. She heard the creaking wheels of Medusa's supermarket trolley getting closer and closer.

Medusa tapped Dakota's shoulder.

'Yes?' asked Dakota, turning to look at Medusa. 'Do you want a cauliflower?'

'No, darling,' said Medusa, 'I don't want a cauliflower.'

Medusa had her cigarette holder clenched between her teeth.

'Potatoes?' asked Dakota.

'No,' replied Medusa, staring intently at Dakota's newly pierced ears, 'I don't want potatoes.'

'Some fruit then?' asked Dakota, backing away from Medusa.

Medusa followed her.

'I don't want anything from the stall, darling,' said Medusa politely, 'although it all looks very colourful. I'm sure the leeks would make a gorgeous soup and the apricots a delicious fruit salad. But you know I'm a poor actress, darling, and can't even afford a pip.'

Dakota continued to back away. This was all part of her plan: to get Medusa as far from her supermarket trolley as possible so Treacle could look inside.

'What do you want then?' asked Dakota.

Dakota peered over Medusa's shoulder.

Treacle was making her way to the supermarket trolley.

'To look at your earrings, darling,' replied Medusa.

'Why?' asked Dakota.

'You know I like to have a look at all new jewellery in the White Flats,' said Medusa. 'Come here, darling.'

Dakota could see Treacle rummaging between the cabbage leaves in the supermarket trolley.

'Why?' asked Dakota. 'I don't understand.'

'Don't ask so many questions, Dakota Pink,' said Medusa. And, with that, she took one last step forward and grabbed hold of Dakota.

Medusa stared intently at the earrings in Dakota's pierced ears while Dakota peered over Medusa's shoulder.

Treacle was still rummaging between the cabbage leaves.

Hurry up! thought Dakota. Hurry up!

'No,' murmured Medusa, letting go of Dakota. 'They're not the right jewels. Not right at all. Not big enough, darling, not big enough.'

'Not big enough for what?' asked Dakota.

'Never you mind,' replied Medusa.

Suddenly, there was a scream.

A scream so loud it made Pat drop a pineapple.

The scream came from Treacle. She was backing away from the supermarket trolley.

'What's wrong?' asked Pat, rushing over. 'What's wrong?'

But Treacle could not answer. She just screamed and screamed.

Medusa ran to her trolley and pushed it away.

Dakota watched her disappear through the crowd.

Treacle was calming down now.

'I'm all right,' said Treacle to her mother. 'Really.'

'But why did you scream?' asked Pat.

'I . . . I . . . just felt like it,' replied Treacle.

'You stupid girl,' said Pat. 'You scared me half to death. Really you did. Now tidy up those cabbages.'

Pat went back to the customer she had been serving and gave her another pineapple.

'Did you see what was in the trolley?' whispered Dakota.

Treacle nodded.

'And?' asked Dakota. 'What was it?'

'It was frightening,' replied Treacle breathlessly. 'The most frightening thing I've ever seen.'

'Then –' began Dakota eagerly.

'Yes!' said Treacle. 'It was a monster! The most frightening monster in the world!'

'Describe it to me,' said Dakota.

They had just finished working on the stall.

All day Dakota had been longing to find out what Treacle had seen in Medusa's supermarket trolley. But it was difficult to talk at the stall while Pat was there.

Now the girls were alone. They had both been paid for their day's work and were walking to Dakota's house so Dakota could cook her mum's evening dumpling.

'It was terrible,' said Treacle. 'That's why I screamed.'

'Terrible in what way?' asked Dakota. 'Describe it.'

'Oh, it was the most –'

'Stop faffing around, toeflake,' snapped Dakota. 'Just give me the facts! What did the monster look like?'

'All I saw was its head. It was green and hairless, scaled like a gigantic snake. Its eyes were black. It didn't have a nose . . .'

'No nose!' exclaimed Dakota.

'No,' said Treacle, 'no nose. No ears either!'

'No ears!' exclaimed Dakota.

'That's right!' said Treacle. 'No ears.'

'How disgusting,' said Dakota, relishing every word of it. 'How big was it?'

'About seven cauliflowers,' replied Treacle.

'Seven cauliflowers,' said Dakota. 'It must only be a baby monster then.'

'That's what I thought!' said Treacle.

'What else did you see?' asked Dakota.

'That's all I saw,' said Treacle. 'Because that's when I started screaming.'

'Well,' said Dakota thoughtfully, 'now *you've* seen it, *I've* got to see it as well.'

'You!' said Treacle. 'But why?'

'I can't have you seeing something I haven't,' Dakota said. 'You know that.'

They went into Dakota's flat.

Dakota's mum, Lucy, was asleep in the Cocoon on Castors. The sound of the front door slamming shut (Dakota was always slamming doors) woke her.

The two girls went into the living-room.

'Evening, Dakota. Evening, Treacle,' said Dakota's mum.

Dakota and Treacle said hello.

'I'm not very hungry tonight,' said Lucy. 'The breakfast dumpling you made me this morning filled me up. Only make me a small evening dumpling tonight, Dakota.'

Dakota and Treacle went into the kitchen.

As Dakota mixed flour and water together to make the dumpling, she said, 'Tonight, Treacle, we're going to break into Medusa's flat and I'm going to see her monster for myself.'

'What!' exclaimed Treacle.

'You heard me!'

'But –'

'No buts,' said Dakota. 'I've made my mind up. I can't have you seeing something I haven't.'

'But, Dakota –'

'Are you scared?' sneered Dakota.

Treacle swallowed hard.

'No,' she replied doubtfully.

'Good,' said Dakota. 'Because I don't want scaredy-cats for friends. If you were scared or if you even hinted that you didn't want to come with me, I would be forced to drop you like a ton of bacon rashers and make another best friend!'

'Oh no, Dakota,' pleaded Treacle. 'Don't say that! Please! I'm not scared and I'm not a coward! If you want to break into Medusa's flat and see her monster then I'll help you. Of course I will.'

'Good,' said Dakota, smiling.

At that moment there was a knock on the front door. Dakota went to answer it.

Pat, Treacle's mother, stood there.

Treacle's mum and Dakota's mum had been friends since they were children, just like Dakota and Treacle are now.

Pat went straight into the living-room and gave Lucy a big hug.

Dakota rejoined Treacle in the kitchen.

'Who was that?' asked Treacle.

'Your mum,' replied Dakota. 'She's probably come to talk about Lassitter Peach and that new novel.'

'Why does everybody read Lassitter Peach?' mused Treacle.

'Beats me,' said Dakota. 'All that soppy stuff makes me feel quite nauseous: girls dressed in pink, handsome men on horseback . . . Yuk! Yuk! Yuk!'

'I know what you mean,' said Treacle. 'I'd rather gargle with jellied eels than read one of those romances.'

'I'd rather tap-dance on a pile of bogies,' said Dakota.

'I'd rather eat stew made out of smelly socks,' said Treacle.

'I'd rather eat a sandwich full of blisters and scabs,' said Dakota.

'I'd rather –' Treacle began.

'All right, all right,' snapped Dakota. 'I'm bored with that now. Give it a rest, tealeaf!'

After Dakota had cooked her mum a dumpling (smaller than normal), made some sausages and beans for both Treacle and herself and fed her pet silverfish, Minty, its nightly dab of toothpaste, the two girls left the flat and went to the square in the centre of the White Flats.

It was dark now and very cold.

They sat by the broken water fountain and looked at Medusa's flat.

'How are we going to get in?' said Treacle.

'I don't know yet!' said Dakota. 'Give me a chance to think, you old biscuit!'

Dakota looked round the empty square at the broken slabs of concrete and the hundreds of discarded supermarket trolleys. Distant footsteps echoed, but she couldn't see who they belonged to. Dakota thought aloud. 'When Medusa looked at my earrings she said the jewels weren't right. Obviously she's after a certain kind of jewel. She said that my jewels weren't big enough. So she needs bigger jewels. What for? We don't know. But . . .' She looked at Treacle. 'That's it!'

'What is?' asked Treacle.

'The plan,' said Dakota. 'You've got to knock at Medusa's door and say you've just seen a big jewel in the rubbish in the water fountain. Then Medusa will come out to look, and while she's doing that I'll sneak in and look at her monster!'

'Why is it,' asked Treacle, 'that every time you make a plan it's always me who does all the hard work?'

Dakota just glared at Treacle.

'All right,' sighed Treacle, 'don't start spitting. I'm going.'

She went to Medusa's front door and then looked back at Dakota.

'Go on!' hissed Dakota, hiding behind a pile of super-

market trolleys. 'Hurry up, you old sugar lump.'

Treacle took a deep breath and knocked.

Almost at once Medusa opened the door.

'Yes?' asked Medusa in her film-star voice. 'What can I do for you, Treacle Duck, my little darling?'

'Pardon me, Medusa . . .' stammered Treacle nervously, 'but I was just looking in the broken fountain . . . and . . .'

'And?' asked Medusa.

'And I saw something sparkle.'

'Sparkle?'

'Yes. I think it must have been a large diamond or something. Will you help me – ?'

'Out of my way!' cried Medusa, pushing past Treacle

and rushing to the broken fountain. 'This could be it! After all these years! This could be it!'

Dakota winked at Treacle and ran past her into Medusa's flat.

Inside it was dark and smelt of cabbages. The walls were covered with cuttings from newspapers. All of them were to do with famous film stars: who had married whom, who had just got divorced, who had won an award, who was seen at nightclubs, who had just been paid over a million dollars to say three lines in a film that cost a hundred million to make. But most of the cuttings were about the jewellery these famous film stars had bought: the largest diamond, the most expensive ruby, the longest string of pearls.

Dakota crept down the hallway and into the living-room. The smell of cabbages grew stronger.

In the centre of the living-room Dakota saw the supermarket trolley. Slowly she crept up to it. She looked inside. Except for a few mouldy cabbage leaves it was empty.

Where's the monster? thought Dakota. What if the monster had heard her coming? What if it was hiding? What if it was waiting to pounce on her?

Dakota looked around the room.

It was dark and full of old furniture. A layer of dust covered everything and there were cobwebs hanging from the ceiling. In one corner a tall grandfather clock ticked loudly and slowly. Above the mantelpiece was a framed photograph of a young man with black hair and a square jaw. He was dressed in a soldier's uniform and he was smiling.

Dakota stared at the photograph.

The young man seemed to be looking at her. His eyes were dark and intense, his skin pale and smooth, and there was something about his smile that made Dakota tingle all over.

A noise!

Dakota spun round.

A noise! A noise from behind the armchair! A strange, scraping sound.

The monster!

Dakota was so scared she couldn't move.

The monster was behind the armchair.

The scraping sound got louder.

The monster was coming to get her.

More scraping.

Then she saw it.

The monster's hideous head appeared from behind the armchair.

It was a few centimetres above the ground and exactly as Treacle had described it: hairless, noseless, earless and green. Its eyes glinted like black ice.

Dakota started to tremble. She wanted to run but couldn't move. She wanted to call for Treacle but her voice had disappeared. All she could do was stare at the monster as it gradually crawled from behind the armchair.

A leg! She saw one of the monster's legs. It was green and like the fin of a fish.

Still it crawled closer . . .

It's going to kill me! thought Dakota.

A hand landed on Dakota's shoulder.

'Got you, darling,' hissed Medusa.

And, with that, Dakota fainted.

6

When Dakota came round she was still in Medusa's living-room. She was propped up in an armchair and there was a blanket over her legs. Treacle was sitting in front of her.

'What happened?' asked Dakota.

'It's your own fault,' said Treacle. 'Don't blame me. You took ages in here. I tried to keep Medusa outside for as long as I could. But when she didn't find a jewel in the broken fountain, she suspected something was wrong and came running back into the flat. I chased after her. We ran in here and we saw you. You were just staring. Staring at the –'

'The monster!' cried Dakota, sitting up and clutching the blanket. 'It was the monster!'

'That's just it,' said Treacle. 'It's not a monster at all.'

'Then what is it?' asked Dakota.

'It's a turtle, darling,' said Medusa, coming into the room with a hot drink for Dakota, 'and not just any old turtle. It's a special turtle.'

Medusa gave Dakota her drink, then sat down on the sofa.

'It's hot cabbage tea,' she said. 'I want you to drink it all, darling. You've had a nasty shock, and hot cabbage tea is the best thing for shock.'

The smell of it made Dakota feel ill, but she took a sip just the same.

Medusa nodded towards the table. 'A very, very special turtle,' she said.

And that's when Dakota saw the whole monster for the first time.

On the table was a large, green turtle. It was the size of a television set.

Dakota's eyes grew wider.

The turtle's shell was encrusted with hundreds of jewels. A galaxy of diamonds, rubies, sapphires, and pearls sparkled in the darkness. It was the most wonderful thing Dakota had ever seen.

'Drink your cabbage water, darling,' said Medusa, puffing at her cigarette holder.

Dakota took a big mouthful. She was so mesmerized by the jewel-encrusted turtle that she didn't notice how awful the cabbage water tasted.

'You're the only people,' said Medusa gently, 'in the whole of the White Flats who have ever seen my turtle. Or should I say, my Oscar.'

'Your Oscar?' said Treacle.

'Yes,' said Medusa, 'my Oscar.'

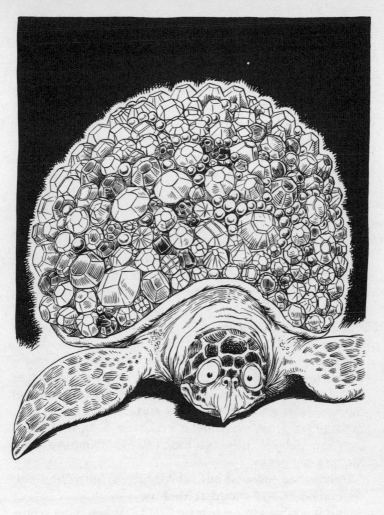

'Tell us,' said Dakota. 'Please tell us the story of your Oscar.'

Medusa smiled at Dakota.

'Why should I?' she asked. 'I know you two girls. Dakota Pink and Treacle Duck. You've called me names like all the other children in the White Flats. You think I'm nothing but a crazy old actress. Stupid old Medusa, you say. Talentless old woman pushing a rusty supermarket trolley and thinking she's a Hollywood star. Why should I tell you anything? All of you, everyone in the White Flats, have made my life a misery.'

Dakota and Treacle felt embarrassed and guilty. Their faces went very red.

'You both know I haven't any money for food,' continued Medusa. 'You've seen me walk past your stall and stare longingly at the cauliflowers and melons. And all you let me have are the dirty old cabbages you leave behind in the gutter.'

'But –' began Treacle.

'Don't bother to explain, darling,' interrupted Medusa. 'There are always excuses for heartlessness. It doesn't bother me any more. I've learnt to live off old cabbage leaves now. I'm quite an expert at cooking them. I make cabbage stew and cabbage pies and cabbage soup and cabbage tea. I can even make a cabbage custard to pour over my cabbage trifle. No, don't worry about me. Old Medusa can get by.'

Dakota had finished her cabbage tea by now. She put the cup down and stared at Medusa.

'But if you've got no money,' said Dakota, 'how come the turtle is covered in diamonds?'

'Who said I've got no money?' snapped Medusa.

'You did!'

'Wrong! I said I've got no money to buy *food*. But I've got plenty of money. And all the money I've got I spend on

jewels. Jewels to cover the shell of my beloved turtle.'

'Where do you get your money?' asked Treacle. 'Do you have a job?'

'In a way,' said Medusa. 'I'm what's called a ghost-writer.'

'What's that?' asked Treacle.

'It means that I write stories for somebody else to publish under their name.'

'What kind of stories do you write?' asked Treacle.

'Love stories,' replied Medusa. 'Stories about what it was like when I was young and in love with the greatest actor in the world.'

'An actor called Oscar,' said Dakota.

'Yes,' replied Medusa softly, 'an actor called Oscar.'

'Oh, tell us,' pleaded Dakota, 'please tell us what happened.'

Medusa took a battered face compact from her pocket and clicked it open. She looked at herself in the mirror and retouched her make-up.

'How do I look?' she asked.

'Very nice,' said Dakota.

'Nice!' gasped Medusa. 'Just nice!'

'Beautiful,' said Dakota.

'Just beautiful,' gasped Medusa, still disappointed.

'Gorgeous,' cried Dakota.

'Gorgeous! Just gorgeous? Oh dear.'

'Stunning!' cried Treacle. 'You're stunning.'

Medusa smiled.

'Yes, darling,' she said, 'I look stunning. I know. I can't help it. Please don't be daunted by my stunning looks. It's just that . . . well . . . some of us are born to be stunning and some of us are born to work on fruit and veg stalls.'

Medusa ran her fingers through her long green hair. Bits of cabbage fell out.

'Very well,' said Medusa, taking a deep breath. 'This is the story of how I fell in love with the most handsome actor the world has ever known.

'When I was a girl I was very talented. By the age of five I could tap-dance, sing, play twenty musical instruments and act the pants off anyone. And if you think I look stunning now . . . well, you should have seen me when I was younger. I was impeccable, darlings. Simply impeccable. I was so talented and perfect that everyone said I was destined to be a star.'

'Did you have good teeth then?' asked Dakota.

'What do you mean?' snapped Medusa.

'Well, all film stars have got good teeth,' explained Dakota. 'I've seen them on the telly. Their teeth are as white as light bulbs. Yours are a little mouldy now.'

'Well, I did have good teeth, if you must know,' said
Medusa. 'Oscar said I had the best teeth he'd ever seen.
But do you want to hear the story of me and Oscar or not?'

'Oh yes,' said Dakota eagerly. 'Please carry on.'

'Very well,' sighed Medusa. 'Now in those days, when I
was young and in love, the world was a beautiful place. It
was full of green hills and thatched cottages and there
were fields of flowers.'

'Where was that?' asked Dakota.

'Why, here!' said Medusa.

'Here!' exclaimed Dakota. 'But the White Flats are here.'

'This was in the days before the White Flats,' explained
Medusa. 'Oh, it was all so wonderful then, darlings. I
can't even begin to describe it. We were all so happy, and
every evening we would go and sit by the river.'

'River?' asked Treacle. 'What river?'

'Why, the canal, of course. You see, when I was young, it was a river with clear, sparkling water full of salmon and tadpoles, and hundreds of swans swam up and down it. Oh, darlings, how can I put it into words. There was music all the time. It was just in the air. Background music, we called it. When you fell in love . . . oh, the music would well up behind you and play beautiful melodies.'

'It sounds just like a film,' said Dakota.

'Why, that's just what it was like, darling. A Hollywood film.'

'Where did you meet Oscar?' asked Treacle.

'We were both auditioning for parts in the same play,' replied Medusa. 'He was going to play the male lead and I was going to play the girl.'

'Did you get the parts?' asked Dakota.

'Yes, we did,' said Medusa. 'Oscar was just wonderful. He was, without doubt, the greatest actor in the world. His full name was Oscar Swashbuckle-Beefcake.

'We spent a lot of time going to the cinema and imagining we were the stars in every film.'

'What films did you like best?' asked Dakota.

'Oh,' sighed Medusa, 'the films that had golden sunsets and elaborate costumes. Films that you could remember. Films that were about love and gave you a good old cry and a happy ending.'

'Those kind of films make me sick,' said Dakota. 'I like explosions and guns and robots and planets blowing up –'

'Oh dear, darling,' interrupted Medusa, 'those aren't films at all.'

'What are they then?' asked Dakota.

'They're just very big fireworks,' Medusa replied. Then she took a deep breath. 'Anyway, on with the story . . . Oscar and I had the rest of our lives worked out. He would become a famous actor, I would become a famous actress; we would both win Oscars, and then we would buy an island somewhere and live happily ever after.'

'So what happened?' asked Dakota.

'A terrible dragon appeared,' replied Medusa. 'A dragon from across the seas.'

'And what did this dragon do?' asked Treacle.

'The dragon wanted to take over the world,' explained Medusa. 'It would fly over one country at a time and lay an egg. The egg would explode when it hit the ground.'

'Sounds exciting,' said Dakota.

'It wasn't exciting at all,' said Medusa. 'It was a nightmare.'

'So Oscar went to fight the dragon,' said Treacle.

'That's right, darling,' said Medusa. 'My Oscar went to fight the dragon. I didn't see him for two years. But we wrote to each other. Long, long letters in which we spoke of Hollywood. Every day I would get up and there would be a letter from Oscar waiting for me. And then, one day, there was no letter. Nor the next day. Nor the next day after that.

'I got very worried. All night I would stay awake and cry, reading all the old letters that Oscar had sent me. And then a telegram arrived. The telegram said that . . . that . . .'

'What?' asked Dakota. 'What did it say?'

'The telegram said that the dragon had captured Oscar and put him in a saucepan and cooked him.'

'Oh, that's terrible,' said Dakota. 'Did you cry?'

'At first I did, yes,' said Medusa. 'But then, that afternoon, while I was sitting by the river, a turtle came up to

me. I had never seen a turtle before, but, suddenly, there it was! And it laid its green head on my lap and looked up at me. And I knew.'

'Knew what?' asked Dakota.

'That my Oscar wasn't dead at all,' replied Medusa. 'That the dragon hadn't cooked him. The dragon had cast a spell on Oscar and turned him into a turtle.'

'I see,' said Dakota softly.

'And I realized something else as well,' said Medusa. 'I realized that I had to cover the turtle's shell with jewels. Only when the shell was completely covered would the dragon's magic spell be broken and the turtle turn back into my beloved Oscar.' Medusa smiled sadly. 'Oh, people said I was mad. That I should be put in a strait-jacket and locked away, or given tiny white tablets to make me sleep. They said the shock of losing my Oscar had driven me insane. But they were wrong. It was they who were mad, not me. Sometimes I believe I'm the only sane one left because everyone else refuses to believe in magic. One day, darlings, I will be reunited with my beloved, and the background music will well up and we'll walk arm in arm into the sunset of Hollywood!'

'So you've worked all your life,' said Dakota, 'buying diamonds and covering the shell of the turtle.'

'That's right,' said Medusa. 'All these years I've written stories for people who want to write but can't.'

'When did you discover you could write?' asked Dakota.

'When I discovered I had no one to love me,' replied Medusa. 'I've written for a whole range of talentless would-be authors. They pay me a little money and I save that money up and buy diamonds.'

Medusa stood up and went to the table. She picked up the turtle and sat down with it in her lap.

'As you can see, darlings,' she said, showing the turtle's

shell to the girls, 'the shell is all but covered now. There's just one little gap left. Just here. I've been searching for the right-size jewel to fill that gap for nearly eight years.'

'So that's why you look at everyone's jewellery!' exclaimed Treacle.

'That's right,' said Medusa, smiling.

Treacle studied the gap on the turtle's shell that needed to be filled.

'Let me see,' said Treacle thoughtfully. 'You need a diamond . . . the size of . . . the size of a pea.'

'That's just what I think,' said Medusa. 'A diamond the size of a pea would just about do it, darling.'

'Who do you write for now?' asked Dakota.

'I don't know if I should tell you that,' said Medusa.

'Oh, please,' begged Treacle, 'please tell us.'

'Well, I write romances for the most famous writer in the world. His name is Lassitter –'

'Lassitter Peach!' exclaimed Treacle. 'My mum reads all his stories. She just sits there and cries for hours. She says there's nothing like a good cry.'

'Sometimes that's right,' said Medusa, smiling.

'Lassitter Peach lives in the Fortress on Dog Island, doesn't he?' said Dakota.

'Why, yes, darling,' replied Medusa. 'He never leaves the Fortress. You have to get to the island by boat, and the river is full of savage eels. Or so rumour has it. Even I've never seen him.'

'How does he get your stories then?' asked Dakota.

'He sends a hooded messenger. Every three months the messenger knocks on my door and I give him the new novel.'

'And you've never seen the messenger's face?' Dakota asked.

'No, I told you, he wears a hood.'

'And the messenger,' said Dakota, 'did he ask you to write stories for Lassitter Peach?'

'Goodness, darling, your curiosity is boundless,' said Medusa. 'Yes, yes, yes, to all your questions.'

'Have you any idea who –' began Dakota.

'No,' sighed Medusa. 'To be honest, I've never even thought about it. He just stands on the doorstep. I give him the novel, he gives me the money, and I buy diamonds. That's all I'm interested in, darling. Really.'

'But –' began Dakota.

Medusa stood up.

'And now you really must go. All this story-telling has gone straight to my head and I need my beauty sleep. An actress has to look her best, you know. Just in case.'

'In case of what?' asked Dakota.

'Talent scouts,' explained Medusa. 'One of them might see me and offer me a part in a film in Hollywood.'

'Can we come and see you again?' asked Dakota.

'Oh yes,' replied Medusa, 'come any time you like, darlings. It is nice to have friends again.'

7

When they had left Medusa's flat, Dakota and Treacle strolled round the corridors and alleyways of the White Flats.

The night was dark and freezing. Distant car brakes screeched and dogs barked. The White Flats echoed with the sound of crying babies, howling cats and, from inside each flat, the noise of a television set.

Dakota looked at the cracked concrete, once white, now yellow, and the hundreds of discarded supermarket trolleys, all gleaming in the moonlight.

'It's hard to believe,' said Dakota softly.

'What?' asked Treacle.

'That all this was once green hills and thatched cottages,' replied Dakota.

'Yes,' said Treacle, 'that's very hard to believe.'

The two girls pushed over a supermarket trolley and sat on it.

'Poor Medusa,' sighed Dakota. 'That turtle must be worth a fortune with all those diamonds and rubies. Fancy having that much money and no one to love.'

Just then there was a noise behind them.

'Who's there?' called Dakota. 'Answer me!'

Footsteps receded into the distance.

'What's that?' asked Treacle nervously.

'I'm not sure,' said Dakota, 'but I think someone might have been eavesdropping on us.'

'Who?' asked Treacle.

'I couldn't see,' said Dakota, still peering into the dark. 'Come on, let's go to bed.'

The two girls said goodnight and went back to their homes.

Dakota found her mum fast asleep in the Cocoon on Castors. Lucy was talking in her sleep.

'Caleb!' Lucy said. 'I bought you a diamond! I bought you a diamond!'

'Forget about him,' said Dakota to her sleeping mum. 'He's gone and we're better off without him.'

Dakota made a hot-water bottle for Lucy, then went up to her bedroom. She got into bed, reached out for the matchbox on the bedside cabinet and looked inside.

Minty, her pet silverfish, stared up at her.

'I love you, Minty,' said Dakota softly, 'I really do.'

She tried to kiss the silverfish, but, although it was big for a silverfish, it was too small for a sloppy wet kiss.

Dakota closed the matchbox, put it back on the bedside cabinet and curled up under the sheets.

For a while she just lay there, comforted by the scarpering sound of Minty running backwards and forwards in the matchbox.

Gradually, though, she drifted off to sleep.

Dakota dreamt she was in a beautiful green landscape. The sky was blue and the sun was shining. She was sitting on the grass beside a handsome young man. It was the man she had seen in the yellow photograph above Medusa's mantelpiece. It was Oscar.

Oscar smiled at her.

Dakota's heart was beating very fast. Her face was flushed and hot.

'You're very beautiful,' said Oscar.

'Am I?' asked Dakota.

'Your hair is as black as the motorway and your skin is as white as bathroom tiles.'

'Thank you,' said Dakota.

'I'm going now,' said Oscar.

'Where to?' asked Dakota.

'There's a dragon to fight,' replied Oscar.

'Oh no!' cried Dakota. 'Don't go! Please don't go! You'll get turned into a turtle and –'

But, as she spoke, Oscar started to turn green. He got smaller and his arms and legs turned to fins. His back arched and became a shell. His ears and nose disappeared and his teeth fell out.

'Help me!' he screamed. 'Help me!'

His face became long and snakelike. In front of Dakota's eyes he changed into a turtle.

Dakota woke. But she could still hear screaming. 'Help me! Help me!' a voice screamed.

At first, as it was Sunday, she assumed it was Henry calling for her to clear the silverfish out of the bathroom again. Then she realized it wasn't.

It was a woman's voice, not a man's, and it was coming from outside the flat, not the bathroom.

Immediately Dakota jumped out of bed and looked out of the window.

Medusa was in the square. She was standing by the broken fountain tearing at her clothes and looking up at Dakota's window and calling, 'Help me! Help me!'

Still in her nightdress, Dakota ran out of the flat.

There was a bruise on Medusa's forehead.

'What is it?' asked Dakota.

'It's gone!' cried Medusa breathlessly. 'Gone!'

'What's gone?' asked Dakota.

'Last night!' cried Medusa. 'Oh, help me! Help me! I was attacked! Knocked out! I woke up to find it gone! Gone!'

'What?' asked Dakota again. 'What's gone?'

'The turtle!' screamed Medusa. 'My Oscar has been stolen and it's all your fault, Dakota Pink! It's all your fault!'

— 8 —

'Now,' said Dakota, 'drink this and tell us what happened.'

She gave Medusa a cup of cabbage tea and sat opposite her.

Treacle was there as well, woken by the sound of Medusa's screaming.

Medusa was sobbing. She took a sip of the tea, then began. 'Soon after you left there was a knock at the door. It scared me at first. I never get visitors, you see. Certainly not at that time of night. I thought it must be some drunks playing a joke. Sometimes they do that. Knock at my door, then run away giggling. They think it's funny.'

'Idiots!' exclaimed Treacle.

'But you opened the door,' said Dakota.

'Yes,' said Medusa, 'I opened the door.'

'Why?' asked Dakota.

'Because when I called through the letter-box, "Who is it?" a voice said it was you.'

'Me?' said Dakota.

'Yes. "Who is it?" I asked. "It's me," said a voice, "Dakota." And it sounded just like you. And so I opened the door, darling. I opened the door. What a stupid actress I am.'

'And who was it?' asked Treacle.

'That's just it,' said Medusa. 'I don't know. As soon as I opened the door someone hit me on the head and knocked me out. I was unconscious for hours. When I came round I was lying on the sofa and my Oscar had been stolen.'

Medusa started to cry again. 'Oh, it's all your fault,' she said between sobs, pointing at Dakota. 'You told someone about my turtle –'

'I didn't tell anyone!' interrupted Dakota. 'Not a soul. When we left here last night we went straight to our flats.'

But Medusa wouldn't listen.

'It's all your fault,' she sobbed. 'All your fault.'

Suddenly, something occurred to Dakota. She stood up and her eyes grew wide.

'Listen,' said Dakota. 'I promise I'll find your turtle.'

'How?' asked Medusa.

'Just trust me! I promise you that I'll find it. Come on, Treacle, we're going.'

'But –' began Treacle.

'Don't argue, coffee bean,' snapped Dakota, and grabbed Treacle by the sleeve. 'Come on.'

Outside, in the square, Dakota looked at Treacle and said, 'You remember last night when we were talking about the turtle?'

'Yes,' said Treacle.

'Well, I was convinced that I heard a noise behind us. When I called out someone ran away. I heard footsteps. Remember?

'Yes,' said Treacle. 'I remember that you –'

'Just keep quiet,' said Dakota. 'Whoever was listening to us stole Medusa's turtle.'

Treacle nodded, afraid to speak in case she was told to shut up again.

'There was something about those footsteps that bothered me then and now I know why,' said Dakota. 'They were the footsteps of someone in uncomfortable shoes.'

Dakota smiled at Treacle.

'Come on, we're going back to my flat,' Dakota said. 'I have a plan.'

The two girls ran all the way back to Dakota's flat.

It was still quite early, so Lucy was fast asleep in the Cocoon on Castors, clutching her now cold hot-water bottle and talking about the long-lost Caleb Pink.

The two girls ran upstairs and along the hall. Dakota rushed to Henry's door and put her ear to the keyhole. Inside Henry was snoring.

'He's usually up by now,' said Dakota, 'but today he's still asleep. And you know why?'

'Why?' asked Treacle.

'Because he's been up all night. Robbing Medusa.'

'How do you know?' asked Treacle.

'Oh, just park your lips for a while and do as I tell you. Go down to the kitchen and bring me all the flour you can find. Then go to the bathroom and fetch me a tube of toothpaste and a bucket of water. Oh yes, and I'll need the

— 66 —

hairdrier as well. We're going to get the truth out of Mr Henry Twig.'

Treacle was about to ask some more questions, but decided against it. She knew that Dakota would get annoyed, so she ran downstairs and started to get the things Dakota wanted.

Meanwhile Dakota took a deep breath and did something she had never done before.

She opened the door to Henry's room.

Henry was asleep in bed. He was curled in a ball, wrapped in white silk sheets, and he was sucking his thumb. Dakota caught a glimpse of his pyjamas and the hairnet. She also noticed that Henry's face was smeared with a thick moisturizing cream and smelt of cucumber and that he had stuffed cotton wool into his ears to keep out the noise.

As Henry slept he mumbled to himself. At first Dakota couldn't understand what he was saying. Then the words became clearer.

'Make me a sandwich, Mummy,' said Henry. 'A banana and sugar sandwich. Put lots of butter on it, Mummy. You know I like your banana and sugar sandwiches!'

Dakota looked around Henry's room.

A model aeroplane hung from the ceiling, a train set ran across the floor. Everywhere she looked she saw toys, jigsaw puzzles, electronic robots, building bricks, a doll's house, tiny soldiers, teddy bears, model cars, spaceships, tanks, a football, a skipping-rope, a cricket bat, a tennis racket, a chemistry set, more dolls.

Dakota hated children's toys. Give her a good rumbling tummy or an insect any day.

Then she saw something else.

It was on the sideboard, between the doll's house and a china doll.

And it wasn't a toy.

It was money.

Lots of money! Piles and piles of ten-pound notes, all held together with elastic bands.

Treacle came into the room. She was holding a large bag of flour, a tube of toothpaste, a hairdrier and a bucket of water.

'Look at all these toys,' whispered Treacle.

'Forget the toys,' said Dakota. 'Look at this money!'

'Where did all that come from?' asked Treacle in a whisper.

'I have my suspicions,' replied Dakota, 'and there's no need to whisper. Henry's stuffed his ears with cotton wool. Now then, have you got all the stuff?'

'Yes,' said Treacle, 'it's all here.'

Dakota opened a bag of flour and sprinkled it over the sleeping Henry. The flour settled on him like snow.

'What are you doing?' asked Treacle.

'Just wait and see,' replied Dakota, sneezing because some flour had got up her nose. 'Come on! Help me! Open the other bags of flour and cover the bed.'

Treacle did as she was told and sprinkled more and

more flour over the sleeping Henry.

When he was completely covered, Dakota got the bucket of water and started to pour it over Henry.

'I still don't know what you're doing,' said Treacle.

'Just shut up, Treacle,' said Dakota.

When all the water had been poured into the flour, Dakota put the bucket down and started to mix the flour and water together, rubbing it into the sheets and blankets.

'Plug the hairdrier in,' Dakota said.

The flour and water had made a thick paste by now, and

Dakota was smothering it all over the sheets. She was making an envelope of bedclothes around Henry. Only his face stuck out of the top. It was as if Henry were asleep in a large, white sausage roll.

Treacle plugged the hairdrier in and gave it to Dakota.

Dakota turned it on and started to dry the flour and water.

'You see,' explained Dakota. 'I've always been fascinated by the way that, when I make Mum's dumplings, flour and water make my clothes go hard. Now I can use that to trap Henry.'

Slowly, Dakota dried out the flour and water. As each section became dry she rapped it with her knuckles. It sounded like stone.

'You're so clever,' sighed Treacle, looking at Dakota.

'I know,' said Dakota, 'I was born that way.'

'But I still can't see why you need the toothpaste.'

'Just park your lips and watch, gravy lump,' said Dakota.

It took nearly five hours to dry out the flour and water completely. By the time Dakota had finished it was early afternoon and Lucy was calling up the stairs, 'Dakota! Cook me a dumpling! I'm hungry.'

So Dakota ran downstairs to make a dumpling for her mum.

When she had made it, Dakota said, 'You might hear some screaming in a minute, Mum.'

'Really?' said Lucy, eating her dumpling. 'And why will there be screaming?'

'Treacle and I are going to torment Henry.'

'I see. Will it take long?' asked Lucy.

'I hope not,' replied Dakota.

'Well, don't worry, dear,' said Lucy smiling. 'I've got the new Lassitter Peach novel that Pat lent me. Nothing bothers me when I'm reading Lassitter Peach.'

Dakota ran back upstairs to Henry's room.

She found Treacle staring at Henry.

'I think he's waking up,' said Treacle.

'About time too,' said Dakota. 'Give me the toothpaste.'

Treacle handed Dakota the tube.

Quick as a flash, Dakota pulled the cotton wool from Henry's ears.

'Wake up, toeflake!' cried Dakota.

Henry's eyes clicked open.

'Dakota!' he cried.

Then he saw Treacle.

'Treacle!' he exclaimed.

The two girls looked at him and grinned.

'Get out of my room!' he screamed.

He tried to move. But his whole body was trapped in a rock-hard envelope of sheets and blankets. Henry's face turned bright red with the effort of trying to escape.

'What's happening?' he cried, panicking a little now. 'Tell me what's going on.'

'I'll tell you all right,' said Dakota, sitting on the edge of the bed and stroking Henry's cheek. 'You're nothing but a crook, Henry Twig. A no-good, dirty ratbag of a crook.'

'That's not true!' cried Henry.

'Yes it is!' snapped Dakota. 'Don't lie to me! Just look at all the toys in this room. Toys cost a fortune these days. How did you get the money for all these presents? Tell me! You haven't got a job, you don't do anything but sleep and look at yourself in the mirror. How did you get the money to buy all these expensive toys?'

'I like toys,' said Henry. 'They remind me of when I was a child. I was happy then.'

'That's no answer!' snarled Dakota. 'You're a thief, aren't you? Confess! You steal things, then buy toys with the money you get. Confess, Henry Twig, or I won't be responsible for my actions.'

Henry thought for a while, his eyes flickering between Dakota and Treacle. There was something about the two girls that scared him. Finally he said, 'All right. I confess. I'm a thief.'

Dakota smiled.

'That's right,' she said. 'Of course you are. And last night you stole something very special, didn't you?'

'What do you mean?' asked Henry breathlessly.

'You stole Medusa's turtle, didn't you?' said Dakota.

'Why do you say that?' asked Henry.

'Because it's the truth, Henry Twig,' said Dakota.

'How do you know?'

'Because your shoes go clickitty-clackitty-click-clock,' said Dakota.

Henry frowned.

'I don't know what you mean,' he said nervously.

'You overheard Treacle and me talking about Medusa's turtle last night. Then you ran away. I heard your footsteps, Henry Twig. I'd recognize them anywhere.

They went clickitty-clackitty-click-clock.'

Henry was shaking.

'Don't hurt me,' he pleaded. 'I stole the turtle. I admit it. But I needed it. The money will buy me a nice new train set with flashing lights and a little engine with real steam and –'

'Shut up, gristle,' said Dakota, standing up. 'You're going to tell me who you sold the turtle to.' She walked over to the sideboard and stared at the piles of ten-pound notes. 'You're going to tell me who gave you all this money.'

'But I can't,' said Henry
'You will,' said Dakota.
'I won't,' said Henry.
'You will,' said Dakota.
'I won't,' said Henry.
'You will,' said Dakota.
'I won't! I won't! I won't!'
cried Henry.

Dakota put her hand in her pocket and brought out her matchbox. She opened it and removed her pet silverfish, Minty. She held it between her thumb and finger and lifted it in the air so Henry could see it.

'You will! You will! You will!' said Dakota, smiling.

Henry screamed.

'No,' he cried. 'Not a silverfish! Anything but a silverfish! Please! Don't!'

Dakota looked at Treacle and smiled.

'Put a dab of toothpaste on his nose,' said Dakota.

Treacle unscrewed the cap and put a large dollop of it on the tip of Henry's nose.

'Help!' cried Henry. 'Help! Mrs Pink! Mrs Pink!'

'Mum won't help you,' said Dakota. 'She's reading one of her romances, and nothing in the world matters while she's doing that.'

Dakota put Minty on the bed just where Henry's feet were beneath the solid sheets and blankets.

'Minty loves toothpaste,' said Dakota softly. 'In a minute it will smell the toothpaste on your nose and start crawling up to have a bite to eat.'

'Take it off!' cried Henry. 'Please! I'll do anything you say! Take it off!'

'Tell us who you sold the turtle to,' said Dakota.

'I can't!' cried Henry. 'I can't.'

Minty started to crawl. It had smelt the toothpaste by now. Its tiny legs scarpered over the solid sheets.

Henry screamed louder.

'Tell us!' cried Dakota.

'No!' cried Henry.

The silverfish reached Henry's knees.

'Help! Help! Help!' cried Henry.

'Where is the turtle?' asked Dakota.

'I can't tell you,' Henry cried.

The silverfish reached Henry's belly.

Henry's screams grew louder and louder.

'Take it off and I'll tell you,' Henry cried.

'Tell first,' Dakota said.

'No,' Henry cried.

'Then the silverfish stays on!'

Minty was at Henry's chest now.

'Eeeek!' Henry went.

Treacle laughed.

'Don't laugh,' Dakota said.
'It's not funny.'

'Yes it is,' Treacle insisted.

'No it isn't,' Dakota said.
'This is serious.'

'Eeeeek!' Henry went.

Dakota laughed as well now.

'There you are,' Treacle said
triumphantly. 'I told you it
was funny.'

'All right,' Dakota said,
'I was wrong. It is funny.'

'Eeeeeek!' Henry went.

Both girls laughed together.

Minty crept on to Henry's neck.

Henry was too scared to scream
now. He lay whimpering like a
baby. Sweat trickled off his forehead.

Minty looked up at Henry's chin.

'It's going to be on your face in a minute,' Dakota said. 'It's going to be on your skin!'

Henry took a deep breath.

'All right,' he said in a tremulous voice, 'I'll tell you.'

Dakota and Treacle waited.

'I took the turtle to the Fortress on Dog Island,' Henry said. 'That's where I take all the things I steal.'

'To the Fortress!' Dakota exclaimed.

'Yes,' Henry said.

'But that's where Lassitter Peach lives,' Dakota said.

'That's right,' Henry said. 'The world-famous romance writer. He's the one that buys all the stolen objects. Especially jewellery. He loves the stuff. But you'll never get the turtle back. No one ever gets into the Fortress. Eeeeeeek!'

Henry screamed as one of Minty's legs touched his chin.

'Take it off!' he cried. 'Quick!'

'Tell us some more about the Fortress first,' Dakota said.

'I'm too scared to talk,' Henry said. 'Eeeeeeeek!'

'That's your problem,' Dakota said.

Henry took control of himself.

'Lassitter Peach is a recluse,' he said. 'He never sees anyone. He's afraid of germs and things. Eeeek!'

'Keep talking,' Dakota said.

'The Fortress itself is made out of barbed wire and broken glass,' Henry continued breathlessly. 'Dog Island is surrounded by infested waters. The eels are larger than normal and very savage. They attack anything. All the pollution in the water has changed them over the years. They're like something from the dinosaur age. It was difficult to row the boat across to Dog Island last night.'

'Why?' asked Treacle.

'Because eels love to eat turtle . . . Eeeek!'

'Keep talking,' said Dakota.

'What do you . . . Eeeek! . . . want to . . . Eeeek! . . . know . . . Eeeek!'

'Tell me how you manage to get into the Fortress. Does Lassitter Peach open the door himself?'

'Oh no,' replied Henry. 'Lassitter Peach sits at his desk all day cutting up magazines and books. He gets through four pairs of scissors a week.'

'Is that all he does?' asked Dakota. 'Just cut up magazines and books?'

'Yes . . . Eeeek!' said Henry.

'But why?' asked Dakota.

'I don't know,' replied Henry. 'He just cuts out photographs of landscapes and puts them on the wall. He's always done it.'

'So how do you get in?' asked Dakota. 'If he doesn't open the door, how does he know it's you?'

'Because of my shoes,' Henry said.

'Your shoes?' exclaimed Treacle.

'Yes,' said Henry. 'The front door of the Fortress is computerized. The computer's memory recognizes my footsteps, you see . . . Eeeek!'

'I see,' murmured Dakota. 'The computer hears your clickitty-clackitty-click-clock and the door opens automatically.'

Henry was going to say 'yes', but all he managed was, 'Eeeeeeeeek!'

'One more question,' said Dakota. 'Where do you keep the boat that takes you to Dog Island?'

'In the canal behind the supermarket,' replied Henry, trying to suppress further 'Eeeeks'. 'I row it down the canal, then out into the river, then across to the Island . . . Eeeek!'

'Good,' said Dakota triumphantly. 'That's all I wanted to know.'

Dakota looked at Treacle.

'Treacle,' she said, 'get Henry's shoes!'

'What for?' asked Treacle.

'I have a plan,' said Dakota.

'Oh dear,' moaned Treacle. 'Not another one.'

Treacle got Henry's shoes and stood waiting.

'Please,' whimpered Henry. 'Take the silverfish off me!'

'No,' said Dakota. 'I'm going to keep it on you!'

'You can't!' screamed Henry.

'I can and I will,' said Dakota. 'You hit Medusa on the head, and this is going to be your punishment!'

'But it's a wicked thing to do,' moaned Henry.

'Yes,' agreed Dakota, 'I suppose it is.'

Dakota and Treacle ran out of Henry's room and went downstairs to see Lucy, Dakota's mum.

'Is that Henry still screaming?' asked Lucy, continuing to read her novel.

'Yes,' replied Dakota, 'he's playing.'

'If that's all,' said Lucy, smiling, 'he's certainly making enough noise about it.'

'Don't let his screams bother you,' said Dakota. 'He might be screaming for some time.'

'Oh, don't worry about me,' said Lucy. 'I've got my Lassitter Peach novel. That'll keep me occupied.'

Dakota and Treacle left Dakota's flat and started walking across the square.

'Where are we going?' asked Treacle.

'To Medusa's,' replied Dakota.

'And what are we doing with Henry's shoes?'

'You're going to put them on, turkey fat,' said Dakota. 'That's what we're doing with them.'

'But why?' asked Treacle.

'Because Henry is the only one Lassitter Peach lets into the Fortress on Dog Island. And it's the sound of Henry's shoes going clickitty-clackitty-click-clock that makes the computerized door open. Right?'

'Right,' said Treacle.

'So tonight we'll get the boat from behind the supermarket, cross the river, cheat our way into the Fortress with a clickitty-clackitty-click-clock, and save Medusa's turtle.'

Treacle stopped walking.

'What's wrong with you?' said Dakota.

'I'm not going to do it,' said Treacle softly.

'You're what!' exclaimed Dakota.

'You heard me,' said Treacle nervously, because she knew this would annoy Dakota. 'I'm not going to do it.'

'You're scared,' sneered Dakota.

'No I'm not,' said Treacle indignantly.

'Yes you are!' Dakota's face turned red with anger. She was shaking all over and saliva began to drip from her lips. 'You're a coward!' she said.

Dakota's voice echoed round the White Flats.

'All right,' admitted Treacle. 'So I'm scared! I can't help it. I just don't want to row across eel-infested water, climb a wall of barbed wire and broken glass, and then have to face the famous Lassitter Peach, and do all this wearing uncomfortable shoes.'

Dakota felt all her anger bubble up inside. She grabbed hold of Treacle and started to shout at her.

This is what Dakota said to Treacle: 'You're nothing but a useless flake of septic toenail, Treacle Duck! You're a tealeaf, a rat-bag, a large green bogy with burst blood-vessels, a lump of sleep from someone's eyes, a teabag that's been used twenty times and is turning mouldy, a carbuncle full of puss and slimy watery bits. You're nothing but bits of toast caught between the teeth of my tale, a throbbing blister in the marathon of my adventures, a rustling crisp-bag in the motion picture of my story, a torn page in the paperback of my ambition, a piece of diced carrot in the recurring vomit of life's throw-ups. You're a boil, a pimple, an ingrowing fingernail, a walking lump of smelly breath, you're the jam that collects between people's toes, the fluff in people's bellybuttons, the wax in people's ears, the dandruff in people's hair. You're all of these things rolled into one with a lot more defects besides!'

After hearing this, Treacle was shaken.

'Now,' said Dakota. 'Will you help me?'

'Of course,' said Treacle, putting Henry's shoes on. 'I'd simply love to.'

'Good,' said Dakota. 'So tonight, my old toeflake, we're going to rescue Oscar the turtle from the barbed-wire Fortress on Dog Island!'

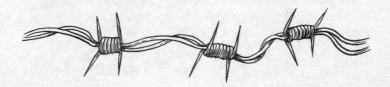

— 9 —

Even at night, when everything else was dark and silent, the supermarket throbbed with life. It was like a gigantic machine, buzzing and pulsating. It was as if all the thousands of supermarket trolleys were alive in there, jostling each other for space, living their own supermarket-trolley lives.

It took ages to walk round the supermarket, as Treacle found it difficult to walk in Henry's pointed shoes. They were much too big for her and extremely uncomfortable, but they made the right sound and that was all that mattered.

Clickitty-clackitty-click-clock, went the shoes.

Finally the girls got to the back of the supermarket. It was quieter there and very dark. Luckily there was a full moon so they could still see.

Dakota stared at the canal, which was full of supermarket trolleys.

'They're everywhere,' Dakota whispered. 'Everywhere you go they've been there first. I don't think there's a place left on the earth that's not full of supermarket trolleys.'

The trolleys gleamed and sparkled in the moonlight.

'It's scary,' Treacle whispered.

'You're such a cornflake!' Dakota said impatiently.

Dakota walked to the edge of the canal. She saw the boat that Henry had told them about.

It was a small, wooden rowing-boat, and it looked very old and weather-beaten. Most of the wood was chipped and splintered and the oars were covered with millions of tiny teeth-marks. These had obviously been caused by the gigantic eels that lived in the murky waters of the polluted river.

'Come on, Treacle!' Dakota exclaimed. 'Let's get going.'

Dakota climbed down into the boat, then helped Treacle to climb on board. It was tricky for Treacle, because Henry's shoes made it awkward for her to keep her balance.

Finally, though, with a loud thud and a scream, she landed beside Dakota. The boat wobbled from side to side and some water splashed inside. The water was dark green and smelt like sour milk.

'I bet the water's poisoned,' Treacle said, shuddering.

'I bet you're right,' Dakota said. 'Now grab an oar and start rowing.'

Carefully, the two girls manœuvred the boat to the

middle of the canal. Then they started to row it down the canal towards Dog Island.

The night was cold and still. They watched the super-market trolleys float by. Some trolleys had been in the water for so long that there was nothing left but rust and slime.

There was lots of rubbish in the canal as well.

They rowed past an old bicycle, then a pram, then a few dolls and burst footballs.

Distant ships blew their horns. They sounded like lost sea monsters singing to each other.

'Isn't it beautiful?' sighed Dakota.

'I suppose it must be,' Treacle said.

Suddenly the two girls were out of the canal and in the wider river.

They rowed past a huge steel ship, tall as a skyscraper. They could hear the men on board yelling and laughing and having a good time.

'Tomorrow they'll be sailing to another country,' Dakota said softly. 'They'll sail across an ocean and visit new places and meet incredible people. They'll eat excit-ing food and swim in clear blue water that's as warm as a bath. They'll collect seashells and wear flowers round their necks and live in houses made of leaves and shark-skin. At night they'll sit round a fire on the beach and cook fish and sing songs and listen to the waves go splash. Doesn't it sound wonderful?'

'Oh yes,' Treacle sighed, 'very wonderful.'

As they moved away from the ship the sailors' songs grew fainter and fainter.

'Do you think there'll be supermarket trolleys where the ship is going?' Treacle asked.

'Oh yes,' Dakota replied confidently. 'Wherever you go there'll be supermarket trolleys. How else can people get their shopping?'

The sailors' voices had disappeared altogether now.

'So many stars,' Dakota said softly, looking up at the sky. 'Do you think there are other creatures in space, Treacle?'

'I don't know,' Treacle replied, wincing with pain as Henry's shoes got more uncomfortable by the minute. Her feet were already covered in blisters.

Suddenly, Dakota gasped. She stood up in the boat and pointed. Her eyes were wide.

'There!' Dakota exclaimed. 'There it is!'

In front of them was Dog Island.

It was like a black sea serpent in the water. And in the middle of the island was the Fortress, a vast building with lots of towers made of barbed wire and broken glass. The spikes of the wire and the splinters of glass glinted in the starlight.

Treacle stopped rowing, momentarily frozen with fear.

'Don't let me down,' Dakota warned Treacle.

Treacle started rowing again.

Dog Island got closer and closer.

Giant eels started to swim towards the boat. They were huge, shiny creatures with gleaming black eyes and tiny yellow teeth.

'They're going to kill us!' Treacle exclaimed.

The eels attacked the boat. Over a hundred of them started to chew and gnaw at the wood. The boat rocked from side to side.

'Hit them with your oar!' Dakota cried.

The two girls lashed out with their oars. A few eels were knocked unconscious. But still the boat rocked wildly and the air was full of the sound of crunching wood.

'We're nearly at the Island now!' Dakota cried. 'Start rowing again! Quick, Treacle, quick! Fast as you can!'

The Island was getting closer.

'We'll sink before we get there!' Treacle screamed. 'And the eels will eat us!'

'Shut up, baked bean!' Dakota cried. 'Just do as you're told! Row!'

As they approached Dog Island the water got shallower and the eels gave up their attack and swam back to deeper waters.

Dakota and Treacle got out of the boat and stood on Dog Island.

The ground was oil-covered gravel. Dakota looked round. Washed ashore were hundreds of supermarket trolleys. It comforted Dakota. Nowhere, not even Dog Island, could escape the influence of the ever-expanding supermarket.

'How do we get in?' Treacle asked, looking up at the Fortress.

Dakota studied the length of barbed wire and broken glass.

'There!' Dakota exclaimed. 'Look! There's a door!'

The two girls walked up to the door. It was made out of metal and was brown with rust.

On the door was a sign. It read:

KEEP OUT
ALL CHILDREN
AND SIMILAR
GERMS

'What a hurtful thing to say,' Treacle said.

'Lassitter Peach certainly sounds like a nasty piece of work,' Dakota said. 'I can't wait to teach him a lesson. Now then,' Dakota continued, grabbing Treacle by the arm and pulling her close. 'All we have to do is get into the Fortress. We know that Lassitter Peach lives alone.'

Treacle nodded.

'Well, go on, then,' Dakota urged. 'Start walking around. You remember what Henry said. The door is computerized. It'll open when it hears Henry's footsteps.'

'But the shoes are so uncomfortable,' Treacle complained.

'You're such a moaning blister sometimes,' Dakota said.

'Blister is right,' Treacle said. 'That's what these pointed shoes are doing to my feet. They're making my toes blister and bulge!'

'Well, if you don't walk round, how else will we get into the Fortress!' Dakota said.

'Why don't *you* wear the shoes?' Treacle asked.

'Because *I* make the plans, that's why,' Dakota replied. 'Now, are you going to walk round, or do I have to hit you round the head with a rusty supermarket trolley?'

Treacle sighed. She knew that she would never win an argument with Dakota. Reluctantly she started to walk backwards and forwards in front of the rusty metal door.

Clickitty-clackitty-click-clock, went the shoes.

'Ouch . . . ouch . . . ouch!' Treacle said, as more blisters formed on her feet.

At the sound of the shoes the rusty door began to open. It made a screeching noise that caused the fillings in Dakota's teeth to hurt.

'It's like magic,' Treacle said.

'Just electrics,' Dakota insisted. 'Come on, let's go inside and sort Lassitter Peach out.'

The two girls stepped through the doorway and into the Fortress.

As soon as they were inside, the door slid shut behind them.

10

Screeech! went the metal door.

'Ow!' Dakota cried, as it made her teeth hurt again.

Then the two girls looked around.

It was very bright inside the Fortress. The ceiling was covered with row after row of fluorescent lights and the floor was gleaming white tiles. Everything sparkled and glistened like a dentist's surgery. It smelt like a dentist's surgery too, an overpowering odour of disinfectant and bleach.

'What's that awful smell?' Treacle asked.

'That's clean,' Dakota said.

'Well, I don't like it,' Treacle remarked.

'I try to avoid it too,' Dakota said.

'Give me Brussels sprouts any day,' Treacle said.

'Precisely,' Dakota agreed.

The walls of the Fortress were covered with photographs which had been cut from books or magazines. They were all of the same thing: a sunlit field of wheat below a blue sky.

'Nice landscape,' Treacle said.

'That must be what Lassitter Peach spends his time cutting out of magazines,' Dakota said.

As soon as she said this they heard the sound of scissors.

Snip-snip-snip, went the scissors.

The snipping sound echoed round them.

'Come on,' Dakota said. 'Let's follow the sound. It'll lead us to Lassitter Peach.'

The sound led them down a corridor. The walls of the corridor were covered with photographs of wheat-fields and skies.

'It's very odd,' Treacle said softly.

'It's getting odder,' Dakota said, pointing.

The girls found themselves in a large room. It had a desk in the middle, a smoked-glass desk with gleaming chrome legs. The top was covered with cut-up magazines and books. There were piles of them everywhere.

And behind the desk sat Lassitter Peach.

He was a short, fat, bald man. He was wearing a white surgical gown, and a white surgical mask over his nose and mouth. He wore rubber gloves, and his feet were covered with plastic bags.

Lassitter Peach was so intent on cutting up another magazine that he didn't notice Dakota and Treacle coming into the room.

Snip-snip-snip, went the scissors.

'Eh, you!' Dakota shouted.

Lassitter Peach screamed and dropped his scissors. He looked up at Dakota and Treacle and he started shaking all over.

'How did you get in?' he asked with a trembling voice.

'Through the front door,' Dakota replied.

'But only Henry gets through the door!' Lassitter Peach cried.

Dakota pointed at Treacle's feet.

'Henry's shoes!' Lassitter Peach screamed. 'What have you done with Henry? Have you fed him to the killer eels?'

'Oh no,' Dakota said. 'Nothing so drastic. The last time we saw Henry he was in bed. Wasn't he, Treacle?'

'That's right,' Treacle replied. 'Tucked up in bed.'

The two girls started to giggle.

'Who are you?' asked Lassitter.

'My name is Dakota Pink and this is my best friend, Treacle Duck. And you are Lassitter Peach, I presume.'

'Yes,' Lassitter replied. Then he added thoughtfully, 'So *you* are Dakota Pink.'

'Dakota of the White Flats,' Dakota insisted proudly.

'What do you want?' Lassitter asked. 'Why have you come here? Have you come to steal my clippings and breathe germs on me? Is that it? Have you come to pollute my nice clean atmosphere? What do you want?'

'The turtle,' Dakota said. 'Medusa's turtle!'

'The turtle!' gasped Lassitter Peach.

'I don't know how you can do it to her,' Dakota said, 'after all she does for you. Writing those awful, soppy, romantic stories.'

'I pay her for them!' exclaimed Lassitter.

'So that makes it all right?' Dakota said.

'Money makes everything all right. I want to be a writer so I pay Medusa. Henry needs toys so he steals things for me. You see, we're all connected. We're all using each other. And money makes things all right.'

There was something gnawing at Dakota's mind. Something she couldn't quite put her finger on. For the moment she decided to ignore it.

'Just tell us where the turtle is,' she cried.

'But I want it,' Lassitter cried. 'It's mine now.'

'Why do you want it? Surely you've got all the diamonds you need.'

'Diamonds!' Lassiter Peach exclaimed. 'I don't want it for its diamonds, you stupid girl. I want to eat it!'

'To eat it!' Treacle cried.

'Why, yes. It's been years since I had a nice bowl of turtle soup. Oh, have you ever had it? It's delicious. You simmer the turtle for three hours, then slice –'

'Have you cooked it yet?' Dakota asked.

'No,' Lassitter Peach replied, 'I was just about to.'

Dakota took a step forward. She stared intently at Lassitter Peach: his bald head, his white surgical mask and white surgical gown, the rubber gloves on his hands and the plastic bags over his feet.

'You're a burst blister, Lassitter Peach,' Dakota said. And she pulled his surgical mask off.

'I'll breathe in germs,' gasped Lassitter. 'Help!'

Dakota pulled his gloves off.

'I'll get millions of bugs!' Lassitter screamed.

Dakota noticed that Lassitter was wearing a diamond ring. It gleamed beneath the neon strip-lights. For a second the dazzling jewel almost blinded Dakota. Then her vision cleared and she studied it more closely.

'Look at his ring,' Dakota said to Treacle. 'How big would you say it was? In Treacleze?'

'Oh,' Treacle said thoughtfully.
'Quarter of a grape.'

'Or?' Dakota asked.

'Two-hundredth of an apple,' Treacle said.

'Or?' Dakota asked again. 'What else?'

'A pea,' Treacle said.

'Exactly!' Dakota exclaimed triumphantly. 'A pea! Just what I was thinking.'

Lassitter Peach was trembling now.

Dakota took a step forward.

Lassitter Peach backed away. He knocked the seat over behind him. It crashed to the floor.

'Afraid of germs, huh?' Dakota sneered. 'Well, I'll spit you to germination if you don't tell us where the turtle is.'

'But I want my turtle soup!' Lassitter pleaded.

'That does it,' Dakota said. 'Treacle! Start spitting!'

The two girls spat in unison at the screaming Lassitter Peach.

Dakota's spit hit his feet.

Treacle's spit hit his shins.

'Stop!' Lassitter Peach cried. 'This is very germy!'

'Then tell us,' Dakota demanded, filling her mouth with spit.

Lassitter hesitated.

Dakota spat as hard as she could. Her spit landed on the diamond the size of a pea.

'All right!' Lassitter screamed. 'I'll tell you! I'll tell you! The turtle's downstairs in the cellar. You go down the staircase and it's the third door on the left.'

Dakota looked at Treacle.

'Go and get it,' Dakota said.

'But –' Treacle began.

'Do it, bacon rind! I've got something to discuss with Mr Lassitter Peach.'

Treacle ran across the room and down the stairs. Clickitty-clackitty-click-clock, went the shoes.

'What do you want?' Lassitter Peach asked nervously.

Dakota glared down at the fat, bald man.

'That ring you're wearing,' Dakota said. 'All my life I've been hearing about a ring. A ring with a diamond the size of a pea. You see, that's what my mum bought my dad.'

There was a pause.

'Don't spit on me again,' Lassitter Peach whispered.

'You're my dad, aren't you?' Dakota said. 'Your real name's not Lassitter Peach at all. It's Caleb Pink. And you married my mum. And you left home blaming me for your lack of talent. You named me after a photograph you saw.

A photograph of a place called North Dakota.' Dakota looked round. 'That's what all these photographs are, aren't they? Photographs of North Dakota.'

'Yes,' Lassitter Peach said softly.

'So, you are my dad.'

'Well, that's a bit blunt, isn't it?' Lassitter said.

'Blunt? How do you mean?' Dakota asked. 'You either are my dad or you're not.'

'Well,' Lassitter said thoughtfully. 'There're other ways of putting it.'

'What other ways?' Dakota asked.

'I'm not sure,' Lassitter replied. 'I'll have to think about it and –'

'ARE YOU MY DAD?' Dakota yelled.

She screamed so loud that the walls shook.

Several photographs fluttered to the floor.

'Yes,' Lassitter said timidly. 'I'm your dad.'

Dakota couldn't speak for a while. She just stared at him. Finally she said, 'Mum always described you as tall and handsome with beautiful black hair.'

'Memory plays tricks,' Lassitter Peach said – or Caleb Pink. 'It's not my fault.'

'So what happened?' Dakota asked. 'After you ran away because all children made you feel ill. I thought you would have gone straight to your precious Dakota and stayed there.'

'Oh, I did,' Lassitter said. 'I caught the first plane. Once I was there I went straight to the glorious wheat-fields that I loved so much. And, while I stood in the middle of a wheat-field, something horrible happened.'

'What?' Dakota asked.

'I started to sneeze,' Lassitter replied. 'Just one sneeze after another. My body shook with sneezes. I couldn't catch my breath. For the first time in my life I started to suffer from hay fever.'

Dakota laughed.

'It's not funny,' Lassitter cried. 'You don't know what it's like to be in love with a place but unable to live there.'

'So you came back here,' said Dakota.

'That's right. I came back here and collected photographs instead. Photographs can't make you sneeze.'

'And you still hated children?'

'Oh, despised them. I only had to see a child playing and I would feel ill. And then . . . and then, one day, a teenager tried to rob me. I was just walking along when up he comes and says, "Give me all your money or I'll chew your face off." I liked him at once. I became friends with him.'

'And his name was Henry Twig,' Dakota said.

'That's right. His name was Henry Twig.'

'So what then?' Dakota asked. 'How did you end up here?'

'Well,' Lassitter began, enjoying the story now. 'I explained to Henry how I wanted to be a writer, but couldn't write. A bit of a problem. Now Henry knows all the tricks in the book. He said we should simply pay someone else to write my book for me.'

'And he found Medusa.'

'She needed the money. Henry got me started, you see. He stole things for a while. Got enough cash for us to live on. When the first Lassitter Peach novel came out it was a success. Sold millions. I made a fortune.'

'And became afraid of germs.'

'That's right. The more money I got, the more I became afraid of dirt and grime and germs and people in general. The only person I could stand seeing was –'

'Henry,' Dakota interrupted.

'That's right. Henry Twig.'

'And you told him to live with Mum and me.'

'Correct,' Lassitter said smiling. 'Right from the beginning he's been living with you. And you know why?'

'Why?' Dakota asked.

'So he could *torment* you,' Lassitter replied with relish. 'Torment *you!*' He pointed at Dakota. 'Leaving you wasn't enough, you see. You had to be tormented day and night! Tormented for what you did to me.'

'But what did I do to you?' Dakota asked, puzzled.

'You took away my talent!' Lassitter Peach shouted. 'You made me a hack when I could have been a genius!'

At that moment Treacle ran back into the room. She was holding the jewel-encrusted turtle.

'It weighs twenty cabbages,' she said.

'Then put it down,' Dakota said. 'We've got some more things to do before we go.'

Treacle put the turtle on the floor, then walked over to Dakota.

'What now?' Treacle asked.

Dakota pointed at Lassitter's diamond ring.

'A diamond as big as a pea!' Dakota said. 'Where have you heard that before?'

'I'm not sure,' Treacle said.

'Well, I'll tell you,' Dakota said. 'I've heard it twice in my life. The first, we won't go into now. But the second . . . the second was from Medusa. She said she needed a diamond as big as a pea to complete the jewel-shell of her turtle.'

Treacle smiled and jumped with glee.

'That's right!' she cried. 'That's what she said! I remember now! I remember!'

Lassitter took a step back.

'You can't have my ring!' he said.

'Why?' Dakota asked.

'Because it's mine!'

'That's no reason.'

'It's reason enough.'

Dakota filled her mouth with spit.

Seeing her do this, Lassitter panicked.

He took the ring from his finger, put it in his mouth and swallowed.

'There!' he said. 'Now you'll never get it!'

'What do we do now?' Treacle asked.

Dakota thought for a while.

Then she smiled.

'I know,' Dakota said. 'Tie him up!'

The two girls jumped on Lassitter Peach.

They pulled the cord from his surgical gown and tied him to the seat behind his desk.

Lassitter was laughing.

'You can do what you like!' he sneered. 'Tie me up and spit at me. But you still won't get the diamond!'

Dakota stared at Lassitter Peach.

'Oh no,' Dakota said. 'I won't spit at you. But I will get the diamond.'

'How?' Lassitter Peach asked.

'Because I know what makes you sick.'

Lassitter Peach's lips started to tremble.

'You do?' he asked nervously.

'I do,' Dakota replied. Then she looked at Treacle. 'Play games with me, Treacle,' she said.

'What games?' Treacle asked.

'Soppy children's games!' said Dakota. 'Like other children.'

'But we hate those sorts of games.'

'I know. Just do it!'

'Tell me why first,' Treacle demanded.

'Because Lassitter Peach isn't Lassitter Peach at all,' Dakota said. 'His name is Caleb Pink and he's my father and children make him feel sick.'

'I was sick once,' Treacle said. 'It was after I'd eaten a mouldy haddock.'

'What were you doing eating a mouldy haddock?' Dakota asked.

'I didn't know it was mouldy at the time,' Treacle replied. 'Mum was sick as well. It was nasty. I don't want to be sick ever again.'

'Well, you won't be if you stay away from mouldy haddocks,' Dakota said. 'Come on! Let's play silly games!'

And with that the two girls started running around the room chasing each other. They laughed and giggled and squealed with glee.

'Catch me if you can!' Dakota called.

Treacle chased after her.

Dakota hid behind Lassitter Peach.

'Oh no,' Lassitter Peach said. 'Don't . . . don't act like children! Please! Oh no!'

Lassitter Peach's face was turning very pale. His lips were trembling and sweat appeared on his forehead.

'I feel very ill,' he said faintly.

'Can't catch me, can't catch me!' Dakota called in a silly sing-song voice.

'Stop it,' Lassitter whimpered. 'Please! Stop it!'

Now the two girls started skipping round the room and singing nursery rhymes.

Lassitter Peach's stomach began to make strange rumbling sounds.

Still the girls sang nursery rhymes.

'Listen!' Treacle said to Dakota. 'His belly!'

'Keep playing!' Dakota cried. 'We're nearly there now! Come on! Let's play leap-frog!'

Treacle bent down and Dakota started to jump leap-frog style over her.

Dakota laughed out loud.

Treacle giggled.

The noise in Lassitter Peach's stomach grew much, much louder.

It sounded like a car engine revving up.

Dakota's childish giggles filled the room.

Then Lassitter Peach's face turned bright red. He sat up and went rigid. The rumbling in his stomach grew louder and louder and louder and louder . . .

Dakota and Treacle stopped playing and stared at him.

The noise in Lassitter's stomach was almost deafening now. It was so loud the room started to vibrate.

Lassitter Peach's mouth opened.

And then it happened . . .

Lassitter Peach was sick.

A jet of thick, steaming, multicoloured vomit spurted out of his mouth with such force that it hit the opposite wall.

Lassitter Peach lay back and stared at the ceiling.

Dakota stared down at Lassitter and there, on his tongue, she saw the ring.

She picked it up and smiled at Lassitter.

'Thank you very much,' she said. Then she looked at Treacle. 'Come on, let's get out of here! Grab the turtle, Treacle, we're going home!'

The two girls ran out of the Fortress.

Outside it was still dark and cold.

'There's the boat!' Dakota exclaimed. 'Over there!'

They ran over to the wooden boat, put the turtle inside, then got in themselves. Dakota grabbed an oar and started to push the boat away from the bank. But the bank was so muddy that the boat had got stuck and wouldn't budge.

'Help me, Treacle!' Dakota cried.

Treacle grabbed an oar and started to push against the mud.

Squelch, went the mud.

But the boat wouldn't move.

'We're stuck here for good,' Treacle moaned.

'Shut it, custard lump!' Dakota snapped. 'This boat is our only escape! We've got to make it move!'

Just then Dakota was interrupted.

A deafening cry echoed across Dog Island.

'CHILDREN!'

The two girls looked up. They couldn't believe their eyes.

Lassitter Peach had slipped out of the cord that had held him prisoner and was staggering through the rusty doorway.

'CHILDREN!' he screamed. 'I'M GOING TO FEED YOU TO THE EELS, CHILDREN! I'M GOING TO WATCH THEM EAT YOU!'

Treacle started to shake so much that she nearly dropped the oar.

'Pull yourself together, teabag!' Dakota snapped.

'But he's supposed to be afraid of germs,' Treacle whispered.

'We've shocked him out of that,' said Dakota. 'Quick! Keep pushing! Otherwise we're going to be a midnight menu for the mutant eels.'

The girls pushed.

Squelch, went the mud.

Lassitter Peach got closer.

'CHILDREN!' he screamed.

'Push!' Dakota cried. 'Push harder!'

Slurp, went the mud.

'Push!' Dakota cried again.

And then the boat moved.

'Push!' Dakota cried. 'Harder!'

The boat moved some more.

Lassitter was nearly at the boat now.

With a loud glugging sound the boat moved away from the bank and into the river.

Lassitter lurched forward.

His fingers grabbed hold of the boat.

Treacle screamed.

'Start rowing!' Dakota cried. 'Quick!'

The girls started rowing.

Lassitter's fingers slid off the boat, but he strode out after them into the filthy, black water of the river. Then the water got too deep for him.

Dakota and Treacle rowed the boat away as fast as they could.

Lassitter Peach receded into the distance.

'CHILDREN!' he screamed after them. 'I'M GOING TO CHASE YOU FOR EVER!' And his voice echoed and re-echoed across the silent darkness of the water. 'CHASE YOU FOR EVER . . . CHASE YOU FOR EVER . . . FOR EVER . . . for ever . . . ever . . . ver . . . er . . .'

11

As soon as Lassitter Peach's cries had disappeared and Dog Island could no longer be seen, the girls stopped rowing. They looked at each other, smiled and relaxed a little.

'What a creep of a man,' Treacle said breathlessly.

'A real toerag,' Dakota said. 'Honestly!'

Both girls were exhausted.

Around them the night seemed unbelievably quiet and still. Dakota looked up at the night sky. The stars were shining brightly and the full moon seemed to be smiling at her.

She looked at the bottom of the boat. The jewel-encrusted turtle was chewing at some seaweed.

Dakota studied the ring with a diamond the size of a pea. It sparkled in the starlight. For a while she was lost in thought. Then she shook herself and said, 'Come on, Treacle. Let's row faster. I'm getting bored with this adventure now.'

Treacle rowed a little faster.

Splash, went the water.

The boat moved into the deep river.

Then they heard a noise . . .

A strange, hissing sound. Like a hundred torpedoes speeding towards them.

'What's that?' Treacle asked nervously.

Dakota peered into the dark.

'I don't know,' Dakota said.

'Where's it coming from?' Treacle asked.

'All round us,' Dakota cried.

The hissing got louder and louder.

Suddenly, over a hundred eels attacked the boat. Their sharp yellow teeth sank into the wood and chewed. Their smooth black bodies thrashed in the water.

The noise of their chewing was deafening.

Dakota lifted her oar into the air. Thirty eels dangled from it. Their skin gleamed in the moonlight.

Dakota screamed and dropped the oar.

It fell into the water and sank without trace.

'What are we going to do?' Treacle cried.

'I don't know,' Dakota said.

'Why have they gone mad like this?' Treacle asked.

Dakota looked over the edge of the boat. The water was a writhing mass of eels. They were even biting each other to get at the boat.

Then Dakota thought of something.

'It's the turtle!' Dakota exclaimed. 'Remember what Henry said about eels liking turtle. They can smell the turtle. That's why they've gone mad!'

Treacle picked up the turtle.

'What are you doing?' Dakota asked.

'I'm going to throw the turtle to them,' Treacle replied.

Dakota snatched the turtle from her.

'Don't be selfish!' Dakota cried.

'But the eels will kill us!'

'Not if I can help it,' Dakota said sternly. 'Now pick up your oar and start rowing. All we have to do is get to the canal. Nothing can live in the canal because it's so polluted.'

'But the boat's sinking already!' Treacle cried.

'Then you'd better hurry up!' Dakota shouted.

Taking a deep breath, Treacle started to row.

Water was seeping into the bottom of the boat.

Eel heads appeared through the holes in the wood. Their eyes were like tiny black buttons.

Treacle screamed when she saw them.

'Shut it!' Dakota cried, hugging the turtle close to her and kissing its scaly head. 'Just keep rowing!'

Water was up to Treacle's ankles now.

An eel swam into the boat and started to nibble at Treacle's feet.

Treacle screamed again.

Dakota reached down, picked up the eel and threw it overboard.

They were nearly at the canal now. But still the eels attacked with increasing ferocity.

Lower and lower sank the boat.

Water was halfway up Dakota's and Treacle's shins.

More eels swam into the boat.

Treacle screamed.

'Shut it, blister!' Dakota cried. 'Just keep rowing.'

She threw the eels overboard.

'I can't stand this,' Treacle said tearfully. 'It's all too much!'

'You haven't much choice,' Dakota said.

When the first current of polluted canal water hit the eels they stopped gnawing at the boat. When the second current hit them they closed their mouths. And when the third current hit them they swam away. They went back into the deeper, less polluted water of the river as fast as they could.

The boat glided into the canal.

But it was still sinking.

'Quick!' Dakota cried. 'We'll have to abandon ship.'

'I can't swim!' Treacle screamed. 'I'll drown and –'

'No you won't! Look! There! A supermarket trolley. Jump on to that! Quick, Treacle, quick!'

Treacle got to her feet and jumped on to the super-market trolley.

Clutching the turtle, Dakota did the same.

Just in time. Because the instant the girls were out of the boat it made a terrible glug-glugging sound and sank to the bottom of the canal.

For a while the two girls stood there, balancing on the supermarket trolley. Around them the water made ominous bubbling noises. The surface of the canal was covered in a layer of oil, and it reflected the moonlight in a kaleidoscope of rainbow colours.

Dakota held the turtle as tightly as she could. Then, taking a deep breath, she leaped on to the next trolley. Treacle jumped with her. The trolley creaked and wobbled beneath the weight of the two girls and the jewel-encrusted turtle. For a while it looked as if it would collapse and send all three of them splashing into the filthy water of the canal.

'Now listen,' Dakota said, once the trolley had settled itself. 'There's a line of supermarket trolleys that leads to the bank. Can you see them?'

Treacle peered into the dark. She could just make out the line of trolleys. They rose from the canal like the bumps of a sea serpent.

'We'll jump from one to the other until we reach the bank,' Dakota said. 'Understood?'

'I'm scared,' Treacle said.

'You're always scared,' Dakota said. 'That's your natural state. Now get jumping before I push you into the mucky water.'

Treacle held on to Dakota.

Dakota clutched the turtle as tightly as she could. Then, taking a deep breath, she leaped on to the next trolley, taking Treacle with her.

Again the trolley creaked and wobbled beneath the weight of the girls and the jewel-encrusted turtle.

As soon as the trolley stopped wobbling, the two girls jumped on to the next one.

Creak, went the trolley as they landed.

'It's going to break!' Treacle cried.

'Keep moving!' Dakota snapped.

They jumped on to the next trolley.

Nearer and nearer the bank came.

'Keep jumping, Treacle!' Dakota cried. 'The turtle's getting heavy.'

They jumped on to the next trolley.

Then the next one.

Then the next.

They were almost at the bank now.

Treacle stopped jumping.

'What's wrong?' Dakota asked, concentrating on not dropping the turtle. 'Move on to the next trolley.'

'There is no next trolley,' Treacle said. 'Look!'

Dakota looked ahead of her. On the bank she could see
the huge back wall of the supermarket. But there was a
little bit of canal water between the girls and the bank. Not
much, but enough if you couldn't swim.

'What are we going to do?' Treacle asked.

'I don't know,' Dakota said. 'It's a bit of a problem.'

'Are we trapped here?' Treacle asked.

'Looks like it,' Dakota said flatly.

'But we can't stand here all night!' Treacle cried. 'It's just
one thing after another! I'm fed up with this! You hear me?
I want it to end.' She stamped her feet. 'I want it to end!'

The supermarket trolley started to wobble.

'Keep still!' Dakota warned.

'I want it to end!' Treacled screamed, stamping her foot
again. 'I've been up all night and I want to go to bed!'

The supermarket trolley wobbled some more.

'Treacle!' Dakota warned. 'Keep still, you stupid old
wart!'

'I'm sleepy!' Treacle screamed.

The supermarket trolley started to break.

Treacle stamped her foot again and slowly the trolley disintegrated beneath them.

The girls started to sink into the water.

Treacle screamed.

The water was cold and slimy and smelly.

Dakota thought as fast as she could.

She put the turtle on the surface of the water.

Instantly it started to swim.

'Quick!' Dakota cried. 'Climb on to his back! Quickly!'

Still screaming, Treacle climbed on to the jewel-encrusted shell of the turtle.

Dakota stood beside her and the two girls embraced.

The turtle remained floating and, with a graceful, solid motion, started to swim serenely towards the bank.

Dakota glanced down to look at the turtle. She saw the back of its green, snakelike head, the tiny bubbles rising from its nostrils, the jewelled shell beneath her feet. The only sound was the splash of the turtle's fins pushing against the filthy canal water.

Moonlight reflected off the diamonds and rubies on the turtle's shell. It was as if the girls were being carried to safety on a magical carpet of light.

Dakota's bottom lip started to tremble.

'What's wrong with you?' Treacle asked.

'Nothing!' Dakota snapped.

'Then why's your lip trembling?' Treacle asked.

'It's not!' Dakota said.

'Yes it is. And there're tears in your eyes. You're going to cry, aren't you?'

'No,' Dakota said. 'Shut up.'

'You're going to cry,' Treacle sneered. 'There're tears in your eyes. I can see them.'

'I'm not going to cry,' Dakota insisted. 'And if you keep pestering me I'll push you into the canal.'

Treacle looked away. She didn't look at Dakota again

until the turtle had crawled on to the muddy bank.

Dakota, however, remained standing on the shell.

'Get off,' Treacle said, impatiently. 'We're safe now.'

Slowly, almost reluctantly, Dakota stepped off the jewel-encrusted shell. She picked the turtle up and kissed its green, lipless mouth.

'Thank you,' Dakota said gently. 'Thank you.'

'Then Dakota licked her lips. They tasted foul. She stared at the turtle and her eyes grew wide with alarm.

'What is it?' Treacle asked.

'It's swallowed some of the canal water,' Dakota cried. 'Quick! We've got to get it to Medusa as fast as we can.'

— 113 —

The two girls ran the length of the supermarket. They were both exhausted and found running difficult. They were wheezing and their legs shook uneasily, their clothes were ripped and filthy, their skin was covered in scratches and bruises, their feet swollen with blisters, and their hair was a tangled mass of seaweed and slime.

The turtle made a coughing noise.

Dakota glanced down at it. The turtle's eyes were turning pale and lifeless. The canal water had poisoned it.

'We'll have to hurry!' Dakota cried.

They turned a corner and started to run down the narrow alleyway that led from the supermarket to the White Flats. It was a long, dark alleyway full of trolleys and empty tin cans.

Suddenly, a piercing scream echoed down the alleyway.

'Ahhhhhhhhhh . . .'

Dakota and Treacle froze.

At the end of the alleyway stood a ghastly white figure. Its arms were outstretched, eyes wide, mouth a black slash in its snow-white face.

'A ghost!' Treacle cried. 'A ghost!'

12

Dakota stared at the spectre, clutching the turtle tight.

Cough, went the turtle.

The white figure took a step forward.

It screamed again.

'Ahhhhhhhhhh . . .'

The two girls took a step back. They were too tired to be afraid.

Treacle tripped over a trolley and fell to the floor.

'Get up, blister!' Dakota snapped.

'It's a ghost, isn't it?' Treacle said, getting to her feet. 'What an adventure this has been: killer eels, Lassitter Peach, a dying turtle and now a ghost! It's all too much! You hear me? I want it to end!'

And with that Treacle started to run towards the howling white spectre.

'Be careful!' Dakota cried. 'Be careful!'

'I'M FED UP WITH IT!' Treacle screamed. 'YOU HEAR ME? I'M FED UP WITH ADVENTURES! FED UP! FED UP! FED UP!'

Treacle jumped into the air and landed on the white phantom.

They both fell to the floor with a crash. Supermarket trolleys tumbled on top of them. For a moment they lay there, struggling and screaming.

Dakota ran up.

'Careful, Treacle!' she cried. 'Careful!'

Treacle was punching and kicking the phantom.

For a moment the phantom screamed and howled and tried to fight back. And then, suddenly, it stopped fighting and started to cry.

This took Treacle by surprise.

She jumped away from the phantom. The whimpering disturbed her more than the creature itself. She stared at the ghostly white face.

'Look!' Treacle exclaimed. 'It's Henry!'

And that's who it was. The white appearance was caused by the flour on his skin and clothes.

He lay there, under a pile of supermarket trolleys, sobbing like a baby.

'Henry Twig,' Dakota sneered, 'how did you get out of your flour-and-water prison?'

'I started to sweat,' Henry explained between sobs. 'And the sweat made the sheets go soft again.'

'And what happened to Minty?' Treacle asked.

'I don't know,' Henry said.

'If you've hurt one leg of my precious silverfish,' Dakota said, 'I'll make you –'

'No!' Henry said. 'I haven't hurt Minty at all. Really I haven't.' Then Henry noticed the jewel-encrusted turtle. 'You've been to Dog Island!' he exclaimed.

'Yes,' Dakota said, smiling.

'And you've seen Lassitter Peach!'

'Yes!' Dakota said, her smile growing wider.

Henry stopped crying and got to his feet. He wiped the tears from his eyes.

'Did you hurt him?' he asked.

'Not too much,' Dakota said slyly. 'Let's just say we made him sick of us.'

'I've got to go to him,' Henry said breathlessly.

'The boat is destroyed,' Treacle said.

'There are other boats,' Henry said, running away from them. He ran down the alleyways towards the canal. 'Lassitter!' he cried. 'Lassitter . . . Lassitter . . . Lassitter . . .'

Once he had gone, the two girls rushed to the front of the supermarket, then into the White Flats and across the square. They ran straight up to Medusa's front door and knocked.

A pause. Then, 'Who is it?' Medusa asked, from inside.

'It's us,' Dakota replied. 'Dakota and Treacle.'

'Have you got the turtle, darlings?'

'Yes,' the girls cried.

Medusa opened the door and let them in. All three of them went into the living-room. Medusa grabbed the turtle from Dakota and kissed it a hundred times.

'Oh, my darling!' she said. 'My precious little darling!'

Dakota took the ring from her pocket.

'Look!' she said. 'A diamond the size of a pea!'

Medusa's eyes grew wide.

'That's it, my dear!' Medusa exclaimed. 'That's it!'

'You'll have to fix it to the shell quickly,' Dakota said. 'The turtle swallowed some canal water on the way here.'

'Canal water!' Medusa said softly.

'That's right. And he's not very well.'

'I see,' Medusa said, looking into the eyes of the turtle.

'Yes, I see what you mean, darling.' Then she smiled. 'Oh, this is such a joyous night, my darlings. I will fix the diamond the size of a pea to the shell and the turtle will become my Oscar again and take me to Hollywood.'

The two girls waited, watching.

'Go on, then,' Dakota urged.

'Oh no,' Medusa insisted. 'I must do it alone.'

'But we want to watch.'

'Well, I'm afraid you can't, darlings. This is a very special, magical moment and it will only work if I'm alone. Now, go back to your mums, there's good girls.'

'But –'

'Please!' Medusa cried. 'There isn't much time.'

Reluctantly, Dakota and Treacle said good night to both Medusa and the jewel-encrusted turtle and left.

'Come back to my flat,' Dakota said.

'Why?' Treacle asked. 'I'm tired.'

'You've got to help me find Minty,' Dakota said.

13

'You look terrible,' Lucy said when she saw the two girls. 'You're dirty and your clothes are torn and you both smell like something rotten.'

Dakota shuffled uneasily.

'And, on top of that, as if that wasn't enough, I haven't had a dumpling for ages.'

'I'm sorry, Mum,' Dakota said. 'Shall I cook you one now?'

'No,' Lucy replied. 'It's still night-time. I can't possibly eat a dumpling while there's a full moon. You two should go to bed and get some sleep, that's what you should do.'

Suddenly, she jumped and lifted her foot.

'Ugh!' Lucy cried. 'Something crawled across my foot. Something with lots of legs!'

'That's Minty,' Dakota exclaimed. 'Quick, Treacle! Help me find Minty! On your hands and knees!'

The two girls got on to the floor.

Dakota saw Minty crawl out of the living-room.

'There it goes!' she cried.

The two girls crawled after it.

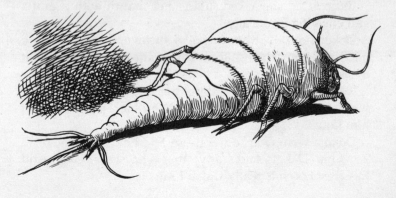

'This is no time to be playing games!' Lucy cried, wheeling her Cocoon on Castors after them. 'Go to bed!'

But Dakota and Treacle were still chasing after Minty.

The silverfish crawled across the carpet towards the coat-stand. Dakota had no idea it could move so fast. Its legs were just a blur as it sped around the coat-stand and towards the front door.

There was a small gap beneath the door – Lucy was always complaining about the draught – and Minty crawled through the gap.

'Minty!' Dakota called. 'Minty! Minty!'

She got to her feet and opened the front door.

'Minty!' she called.

But all she saw was Lassitter Peach.

Lassitter stood on the doorstep. His face was pale and his eyes were still wide and bloodshot. His legs were shaking and, were it not for Henry, who was holding him up, Lassitter would have crashed to the ground.

'He's got a fever,' Henry said breathlessly. 'I found him floating in the river. He was calling your name, Dakota.'

Lucy wheeled her Cocoon on Castors forward and peered closely at the man Henry was holding. Her face became rigid, expressionless, and her fingers delved into the bowl of peanuts attached to the side of her chair.

'Who is it?' she asked, filling her mouth with peanuts and chewing frantically.

Dakota looked at her mum. A strange, nervous feeling filled her stomach and, for a while, she didn't know what to say.

'Well?' Lucy asked, filling her mouth with another handful of peanuts. 'Who is it? Why has Henry brought him here?'

Dakota went over to her mum and held her hand.

'Mum,' Dakota said softly, 'this is Lassitter Peach. And Lassitter Peach is really Caleb Pink.'

Lucy spat out the peanuts.

'I knew something was wrong!' she cried. 'All night I didn't want to think about it!'

Lucy grabbed hold of the steering wheel and drove the Cocoon on Castors through the door, pushing Lassitter Peach back off the doorstep and into the night-time square.

'Owwwwwwww!' Lassitter moaned.

'I'll give you "Owwwwwwww",' Lucy snapped.

She nudged Lassitter back further. They were well into the square now and their voices echoed as they spoke.

Lucy poked Lassitter in the chest.

'I remember you as tall, handsome, muscular, charming, with a shock of black hair and a golden suntan,' she said.

'Lucy . . .' murmured Lassitter. 'Let me explain –'

'Shut up!' Lucy snapped. 'To think I've waited all these years for you to come back to me. How memory plays tricks! Why, you're not handsome at all, are you?' And she poked him in the chest again. 'Are you?'

'No,' Lassitter replied softly.

'You're bald, aren't you?' Lucy asked.

'Yes,' Lassitter said.

'And fat!'

'Yes.'

'And small!'

'Yes.'

'And pale!'

'Yes.'

'And you've got about as much charm as a toenail in a corned-beef sandwich.' And Lucy poked him again even harder than before. 'Haven't you?' she cried. 'Haven't you?'

'Yes,' Lassitter cried, 'yes, yes, yes. I'm bald, fat, small and charmless.'

'And you're a writer as well . . .'

At this, Dakota rushed up and told her mum about Medusa. How she had written the stories and not Lassitter.

Lucy's eyes grew narrow with anger.

'You can't even be talentless honestly!' she cried. 'Why, you're a worm, Caleb Pink – or Lassitter Peach, whatever you call yourself – you're a mouldy tangerine, a maggot in a dumpling . . .' Lucy started to get to her feet. 'You're a baked bean, a soggy biscuit, a rotting cornflake . . .'

Dakota and Treacle stared in wonder as Lucy stepped forwards out of the Cocoon on Castors.

'You're a . . . a . . . a . . .' Lucy went on, trying to think of an insult. 'You're a . . . a . . . a . . .'

'A TOEFLAKE!' cried Dakota and Treacle in unison.

'That's it!' Lucy cried triumphantly. 'You're nothing but a toeflake. You hear me? A TOEFLAKE!'

Dakota and Treacle squealed with glee.

'All these years I've been stuck in that thing,' said Lucy, pointing at the Cocoon on Castors. 'Stuck there, waiting for you. What a fool I've been.'

Lucy started pushing the Cocoon on Castors across the square towards the broken water fountain. It was the first time the Cocoon's wheels had rolled over concrete and they started squeaking. The squeaking was very loud and echoed round the White Flats.

'Help me!' cried Lucy. 'Dakota! Treacle! Help me! I want to throw the Cocoon in the water fountain with all the other rubbish.'

The two girls rushed over and helped lift the Cocoon. It was extremely heavy but, finally, they managed to get it into the water fountain.

'BRING ME MATCHES!' cried Lucy.

Dakota ran back to the flat to find some.

By now the noise had woken everyone in the White Flats. They stumbled into the square – still in their pyjamas and nightdresses – and stared at Lucy. It was the first time many of them had seen her out of her Cocoon.

Pat, Treacle's mother, rushed over to Lucy.

'Lucy!' she cried. 'You're walking! It's a miracle! What's happened?'

'Him!' Lucy cried, pointing at Lassitter, who was still in Henry's arms.

Pat looked closer.

'Goodness,' she said. 'It's . . . it's your husband, isn't it?'

'That's right,' Lucy said. 'That small, fat, bald, pale,

charmless, not to mention talentless, man is my husband.'

Dakota had found a box of matches by now and rushed up to Lucy and gave it to her.

'Thank you,' said Lucy, opening the box and taking out a match. 'WATCH, EVERYONE!' she cried, her voice echoing round the White Flats. 'WATCH! THIS IS GOODBYE TO BAD MEMORIES!'

The White Flats became very still.

Lucy struck the match and threw it into the fountain.

For a moment nothing happened. Then a flame appeared on the cushion of the Cocoon on Castors. The flame grew bigger and brighter and it started to crackle and smoke. Suddenly, the whole fountain burst into flame.

'I'm free now!' cried Lucy. 'I'm never going to get trapped in a cocoon again.'

Lucy embraced Pat and the two women started to dance.

Other people started to dance as well. Everyone living in the White Flats laughed and cheered and congratulated Lucy. The square became one big party.

Dakota looked around her.

The fire illuminated everything with a red, flickering glow. The yellow dullness of the walls was transformed into a shimmering orange. The heat from the fire made the Flats as warm as a tropical night and the sparks like a million fireflies.

The blaze transformed the White Flats. Dakota had never seen them look so beautiful. And, from where she stood, just in front of the fire, her shadow became huge. Her shadow was so big it covered half the White Flats.

Another shadow appeared beside her.

Dakota turned to see Treacle.

'Well,' said Treacle. 'What a night.'

'A magical night!' Dakota said.

14

The next morning there was nothing left in the broken water fountain but cinders.

Dakota stared at them for a while, then went to Medusa's flat. She knocked at the door, but there was no answer. Pushing the door gently, it swung open.

'Medusa?' Dakota called. 'Medusa.'

But there was no reply.

Dakota went inside.

It was dark and still smelt of cabbages. Dakota looked everywhere but there was no sign of Medusa. Both she and the jewel-encrusted turtle had gone.

Dakota stood in the living-room and glanced up at the photograph of Oscar. He still looked brave. She smiled at him.

Treacle rushed in.

'Where's Medusa?' Treacle asked.

'Gone,' Dakota replied softly.

'Gone?' Treacle asked. 'But where?'

'Gone with Oscar,' Dakota replied. 'Last night she must have put the diamond the size of a pea on to the turtle's shell. The turtle turned back into Oscar and he has taken her away.'

'Where to?' asked Treacle.

'Hollywood, of course,' Dakota replied, turning to leave the room.

Dakota and Treacle walked out of the flat, across the square and sat beside the broken fountain.

For a while they sat in silence. The air was still heavy with smoke. The White Flats had been scorched by the previous night's fire and everything smelt like burnt toast.

Then Dakota heard a rustling noise coming from the

blackened cinders in the water fountain.

Rustle, rustle, went the burnt rubbish.

Dakota rummaged in the blackened remains.

Minty ran into her hands.

'Minty!' Dakota cried. 'Minty! You're still alive! I thought you'd gone up in smoke.'

Treacle stood up and kicked at the fountain.

'What's wrong with you?' Dakota asked. 'If you're jealous because I've got lots of money now, don't be. Mum says that the money from all of Lassitter Peach novels belongs to Medusa. So we're just looking after it for her until she –'

'It's not the money,' interrupted Treacle.

'Then what is wrong with you?' Dakota asked.

'I think you like that stupid fat silverfish more than me,' Treacle complained. 'After all we've been through – breaking into Medusa's flat, rowing down the canal, cheating our way into the barbed-wire Fortress, stealing the turtle back, getting the diamond the size of a pea, fighting the mutant eels, struggling with a ghostly Henry – after all that, you're more pleased to see Minty than you are me.'

'Oh, that's stupid, Treacle,' Dakota said, putting the silverfish in her pocket and standing up. 'You know I like you more than anything else in all of the White Flats.'

Dakota gave Treacle a big hug.

'You're my best friend,' said Dakota.

'And you're my best friend,' said Treacle.

The two girls sat next to each other and looked around the square.

Lucy was just going to the supermarket to get some shopping. Lassitter – or Caleb Pink – was with her. He was sneezing loudly, one thunderous sneeze after another.

Henry Twig walked beside him, pushing a supermarket trolley. He wasn't wearing any shoes, because his clickitty-clackitty-click-clock ones had been ruined the night before.

'Hello, Mum,' called Dakota.

Lucy waved back and smiled.

'I've never seen Mum look so happy,' Dakota said as she watched them go to the supermarket. 'Mind you, I think Caleb's sneezing is soon going to get on everyone's nerves. Living in that germ-free Fortress for so long has made him allergic to nearly everything. He's sneezing worse here than he ever did in the wheat-fields of North Dakota. Funny the way things work out.' Then she looked at Treacle. 'What's wrong now?' asked Dakota, noticing Treacle's frown.

'Tell me,' Treacle said softly. 'Do you believe it?'

'Believe what?' Dakota asked.

'About the turtle changing back into Oscar and taking Medusa to Hollywood.'

Dakota thought for a while. She remembered how the White Flats had looked the night before, the way the fire had made everything look so magical. Now the White Flats were anything but magical: scorched walls, supermarket trolleys, a sneezing Caleb, a shoeless Henry and a burnt water fountain.

'Yes,' said Dakota. 'I believe it.'

'I don't,' said Treacle. 'Not really.'

'Well, that's why . . .' Dakota said.

'Why what?'

'You'll always be a toeflake!' Dakota cried.

If you enjoyed *Dakota of the White Flats*, turn the page and read the first chapter of Philip Ridley's exciting book *Kasper in the Glitter* . . .

'I'm getting worried now,' Kasper mumbled to himself. He looked out of the window at the setting sun. 'Good heavens, it's hard to concentrate on cooking when I'm this bothered.'

Kasper was in the kitchen making a Banoffi pie.

Now – just in case you don't know – Banoffi is one of the most delicious pies ever invented. It's made with sliced bananas, gooey toffee, and topped off with coffee-flavoured cream, chocolate granules, and a large dollop of marmalade.

The marmalade, to be honest, is Kasper's own particular addition to the recipe. He says it gives the dish a much needed tang. And he should know. After all, nobody could have made as many Banoffi pies as ten-year-old Kasper Whisky.

Banoffi pie helps cheer Pumpkin up, you see. And as Pumpkin – that's Kasper's mother – needs a lot of cheering up, it follows that Kasper has made a lot of pies.

'You make the best pie in the whole world, honey,' Pumpkin often told him.

'Not today I don't!' said Kasper, remembering her words. 'All this worry has made me slice the banana too thick and mix the toffee too thin and leave lumps in the cream. And as for the marmalade . . . well, there is none!'

Marmalade was one of the things on Pumpkin's shopping list.

That's where Pumpkin was now: shopping.

And she was late coming back!

'Where can Pumpkin be?' Kasper wondered. 'She's never been this late before. But I mustn't get flustered! That won't help! Best keep busy! Let's see . . . the Banoffi pie's finished – all except the dollop of marmalade, of course. I'll put it in the fridge to keep cool. Now what shall I do? I know! I'll clean the sunbeds!'

Now, most houses don't have sunbeds in them, I'm sure you'll agree. But Kasper's house wasn't like most houses. In fact, it wasn't like any other house I've ever seen.

Years ago, you see, Pumpkin had turned the front of the house into a beauty salon. She'd installed not just sunbeds, but hairdryers, couches and piles of magazines, and called the place 'SPARKLE PLENTY'. There was a big yellow neon sign saying as much above the front door. All day it would flash on and off, and – at night – it would light up the street.

When there was a street to light up, that is.

Because just as the salon was becoming really successful, men in bulldozers came along. For months and months they knocked down houses and streets. They said they were going to build new ones. But . . . they never did.

They just went away.

Leaving a wasteground with only one thing remaining: the house where Pumpkin and her newly born Kasper lived.

So now you understand why I say it wasn't like any other house I'd ever seen.

Come to think of it, Kasper didn't look like any other boy I'd ever seen either.

His suit was yellow.

His shirt was lemon yellow.

His bootlace tie: canary yellow.

Kasper was nothing but yellow, yellow, yellow from head to foot.

And I mean that literally, because his hair (which was smoothed flat and hard with a mixture of sugar and water) was golden blond (which is almost yellow) and his shoes (which were very pointed) were mustard yellow.

Yellow was Pumpkin's favourite colour.

Most things in the house had been painted yellow. Including the sunbeds, which Kasper was now dusting.

'Perhaps Pumpkin's lost,' he said. 'Perhaps she'll never come back . . . Oh, I mustn't think like that! Keep busy! That's the answer!'

So, after cleaning the sunbeds, he dusted the hair-dryers.

Then swept the floor.

Then polished the mirrors.

And he was just about to tidy the magazines, when he glanced out of the window and saw –

'Stars! Good heavens, I'm getting really worried now! If it gets much darker Pumpkin won't be able to find her way back. I'd best turn the sign on!'

Kasper flicked a switch by the front door, then rushed out into the garden.

The 'SPARKLE PLENTY' sign was flashing, making the house look like a lighthouse in a vast sea of rubble. Kasper looked at The City in the distance.

It was on the other side of the wasteground, the lights in its tall buildings glimmering against the twilight sky. Kasper often wondered what it must be like to live in The City.

To have people buzzing around you all day and hear the roar of traffic outside your bedroom window. But he tried not to dwell on it too much. Pumpkin hated The City and got upset every time Kasper talked about it.

In fact, Kasper had never so much as stepped beyond the fence that surrounded his house.

Again, Pumpkin would get upset if he did.

So now Kasper stood in the garden, staring at The City, and saying to himself, 'I'm getting really, really worried now! Perhaps Pumpkin's been hurt and . . . No! Mustn't think like that. Keep busy! Let's see . . . I'll water the roses!'

The house was surrounded by a forest of roses. There were rose trees in every corner, climbing roses across the side of the house and along the fence, and rose bushes nearly everywhere else.

And the colour of the roses?

Yellow, of course.

'Stolen roses!' Kasper gasped. 'Here! Five or six roses have been picked. And here! Three or four broken stems. It's the fifth day in a row roses have gone missing. It must be happening at night. No one could get into the garden during the day without me seeing them. But who? Or what?'

And that's when he heard a voice.

'I think I've broken a fingernail, honey,' it said.

'Pumpkin!' cried Kasper. 'You're home!'

Continued in *Kasper in the Glitter*,
also published in Puffin Books

Also available by Philip Ridley in Puffin

MERCEDES ICE

On the very day that Rosie Glow is born, the foundation stone for a new building is laid. As she grows up, so the magnificent tower grows too, as high as the clouds, casting its gloomy shadow over everything. Rosie has only one desire – to live on the top floor of the building known as Shadow Point.

But the reality of life there is very different to her dreams. The shining concrete soon starts to buckle and crack and the gleaming windows grow grimy with dirt. Into this colourless decay comes Mercedes Ice, the Prince of Shadow Point. He can have anything he wants – until the day he asks for the impossible: colour.

An intriguing and surprising fable about love and dreams from award-winning author Philip Ridley.